Letters to
Christian
Ambassadors

Letters to
Christian
Ambassadors

Introduction

Long ago I heard an insight someone offered about being a Christian that I have never forgotten. Here it is: You may be the only Bible some people ever read.

No single phrase I can think of captures as artfully what it means for you to be an ambassador for Christ. To the majority of non-Christians in your life, you are their link to the only truth that can impart eternal life.

You are like the Corinthians who Paul referred to as "our letter...known and read by all men... cared for by us, written not with ink, but with the Spirit of the living God, not on tablets of stone, but on tablets of human hearts" (2 Cor. 3:2-3).

Your life is a letter. *Your* life is read by all men. *Your* life is written not with ink, but with the Spirit of the living God.

Further, you are *our* letter, cared for by *us*, all of us at Stand to Reason who work hard on your behalf. That is why I write you regularly with affection in my heart, "exhorting and encouraging and imploring...you as a father would his own children" (1 Thess. 2:11).

So as a kind off spiritual father, I am always looking for new ways to help you shine for those who only know about Christ through you. I know yours is a weighty responsibility, but in the enclosed letters I offer some ideas that might help.

Affectionately,

Greg

Two Simple Things Make All the Difference

Do you know the survival rate for airplane accidents? You won't believe it. Take a guess right now. I bet you won't be anywhere close.

On average, ninety-six out of every 100 people involved in airplane mishaps survive the ordeal. Amazing, isn't it? Even with serious accidents, as long as there was some chance of surviving, three-quarters of the passengers get out alive.[1]

And here's another shocker. Many of the people who do perish *could* have survived, but didn't. So what makes the difference? If you guessed panic, you'd be wrong. Yes, panic kills, but it almost never happens in desperate situations like airplane disasters, earthquakes, or terrorist attacks like 9/11.

Most people don't panic. They freeze. They do nothing, because they don't know what to do. And that's what kills them. Usually, two things make the difference between life and death: planning and action.

Since I learned those statistics, my preparation at the beginning of flights has completely changed. Before, I never paid attention to things like exits, flight attendant emergency instructions, or reviewing the safety card. What was the point? If something went wrong, I figured, I was a goner anyway.

Now I know differently. I note the exits and try to get a seat close to one (seats two to five rows away are the safest). I review the safety card so I know how each emergency exit door on the plane works. I am fully alert with my seatbelt tight and my shoes on during the most vulnerable times—the first three and the last eight minutes of any flight.

And I have a plan in case something goes wrong, a plan I review every flight at take-off and just before landing.

Here's the point: Our preparation is different when we have an expectation that preparation will make a difference. And when we have a *plan*, we are more likely to *act*.

That's why having the first two Columbo questions handy—"What do you mean by that?" and "How did you come to that conclusion?"—makes being Christ's ambassador so much easier. Whatever situation you face, you have a basic game plan at the ready.

But you can do better than that. When I speak, I sometimes ask audiences, "How many people here hate taking tests?" Virtually every hand shoots up. Then I ask how many mind taking tests *when they know the answers*. The hands go down. Tests aren't the problem. Instead, we fear being immobilized by our ignorance.

This reminds me of Yogi Berra's memorable malaprop, "I wish I had an answer to that, because I'm tired of answering that question." Yogi would have been less "tired" if he had planned ahead to be ready for that vexing question when it inevitably popped up.

So, I want you to think for a moment about the most vexing challenge you as an ambassador for Christ face from a skeptic, that issue you dread being mentioned, the question you hope never comes up. Next, do some research and develop a specific plan of response to it that is tactically sound.

I used to flinch at the problem of evil. It's a popular challenge that is emotionally compelling and difficult to work through in a short conversation, even if you know the intricacies of the issue. So I developed a short game plan.

I know the first question I'll ask when someone raises the issue—"So you believe in objective evil then?" (If they don't, the challenge disappears. No objective evil; no problem of evil. This roots out the relativists.)

I also know my follow-up question—"What do you mean by 'evil'?"

I don't want them to give me examples of evil—murder, torture, wanton suffering. I want them to tell me what it is that makes those things objectively evil in the first place. This leads to a discussion about transcendent moral law and the need for a transcendent moral law Maker. God has to exist before anyone can even raise the objection about evil.

When people ask if Jesus is the "only way" (another awkward challenge), I say, "Well, that's what Jesus thought. Do you think He had any insight into spiritual things?" Now the ball is in their court, but this time they have to take on Jesus, not me.

In the last chapter in my *Tactics* book, I mentioned a Marine Corps training slogan: The more you sweat in training, the less you bleed in battle. This is the same lesson we have been talking about. The easiest way to beat fear is to remember two simple concepts that will save your bacon in just about any disaster: preparation and action.

I hope my encouragement to *plan* so you can *act* will bear fruit as you seize opportunities to engage as an ambassador. Remember, no one fears a test they know the answers to.

In His care,

Greg

A Struggle and a Solution

Let me start with a frank admission: Prayer is difficult for me. Some things come easily, but prayer is not one of them. Of course, this does not make prayer optional in the least. It simply means I have to work harder at it to be consistent and effective.

I suspect there are many Christians just like me in this regard. Maybe you would include yourself in that group. If so, these thoughts on prayer might be helpful to you.

Here is a key observation that has helped improve my own prayer life: *Prayer is harder when it is rambling.* It is harder for the person praying, and it is harder for those listening when prayer is in a group.

One of my frustrations when praying with others is that Christians often don't pray intelligibly. We tell young Christians who are unaccustomed to prayer to simply talk normally when speaking to God. "Prayer is conversation," we say. And it is.

That is what we *tell* them, but that is not what we *do* when we pray with them. When it comes to God, our normal way of speaking often goes out the window.

We lace our prayers with contrived Christian mumbo jumbo (some have called it "Christian psycho-babble"). We insert useless words like "just" in virtually every phrase. Then we use the words "Lord," "Father," and "Jesus" as if they were punctuation marks. In short, we talk to God in ways we wouldn't think of talking when speaking with any other intelligent person.

This habit is hard to break. I know from personal experience. But I have a solution that has helped me trim down the nonsense. I have instructed our staff at STR that when we meet for prayer, we pray according to the acronym SIP: specifically, intelligibly, and persuasively.

I take this cue from the prayers in the Bible (Daniel 9:3-19 is an example). Biblical prayers have content, clarity, and power. There is no spiritual blather. In many cases, they include *reasons* why God should act, as if the person praying were persuading Him of something He wouldn't do apart from their entreaty.

Sometimes the reasons are based on the need. Other times they are based on God's character or what might happen to His reputation if He ignored the request (this was a favorite practice of Moses).

These are the things you would normally— and quite naturally—say if you were speaking to someone of importance making request for help or provision. You'd explain your need, why you need it, and why your request should be granted.

I think we should do the same with God. We should pray in full sentences, intelligibly, with complete thoughts. Our prayers should include clear, specific requests, and straightforward, genuine expressions of feeling and thanks. We should also give reasons why God ought to respond to our appeals.

Some people find that occasionally writing their prayers out is helpful. It forces them to put more clarity and substance into their entreaties.

I hope you did not skim over the phrase above, "I have instructed our staff at STR...." Since I am the spiritual head of Stand to Reason, this is one of the ways I mentor those on our team. If you are in leadership, this applies to you, too.

I have often wondered why those training leaders in their youth group (for example) apparently never taught the worship team how to pray in public. Those who lead prayer for the group are examples to the rest. If they model good prayer habits, others will likely follow their lead. But the same works in reverse, too.

So, if you have spiritual leadership responsibilities of any sort—with your family, your church, or accountability group—you may want to do two things in response to what I've said here.

First, apply the SIP principle to your own prayer life. Train yourself to pray specifically, intelligibly, and persuasively. Even if prayer is not as difficult for you as it is for me, I think you'll find that this practice will help your prayers be more powerful and fulfilling.

Second, instruct those in your spiritual charge how to pray "conversationally." Then model it for them when you pray together. There is no need to be pious, just clear and genuine. In this way, you will be helping yourself and also those around you.

We use the SIP principle at STR staff meetings when we pray together. I use it in my own personal prayer life. You can use it, too, to make your times of prayer meaningful and relevant.

Warmly,

Greg

A World View or a View of Reality?

I noticed something stunning a few years back while paging through Frederick Copleston's landmark work, *A History of Philosophy*, for a class. Virtually every major thinker in the history of western civilization from the beginning of the first millennium until the 19th century was a deeply committed Christian theist.

The list is impressive: Irenaeus, Eusebius, Augustine, John Duns Scotus, Anselm of Canterbury, Thomas Aquinas, William of Ockham, Rene Descartes, Gottfried Leibniz. It isn't until the Enlightenment that God and the Bible are not a standard part of the philosophic equation.

For 18 centuries, those who thought deeply and carefully about reality did so with the conviction that God was real, that Jesus was His messiah, and the Gospel was the power of God to change lives.

Let me tell you why this discovery was so important to me. As you may know, I used to think I was too smart to be a Christian. As an Honors College student in pre-law at Michigan State University, I thought Jesus was for socially unacceptable fools who needed someone to do their thinking for them.

So when I was drawn into the Kingdom, it was an epiphany of sorts to realize how wrong I was. Early on I discovered Francis Schaeffer and his seminal trilogy: *The God Who Is There*, *Escape from Reason*, and *He Is There and He Is Not Silent*. Then there was C.S. Lewis, Josh McDowell, J.P. Moreland, and a host of others since.

These luminous minds convinced me that Christianity is worth thinking about. It's a phrase I know you've heard me use often. I open my talks at radically liberal schools like Cal Berkeley, UC San Diego, UCLA, and Ohio State with those words.

It's become almost synonymous with STR. In fact, I frequently use both phrases together: "Stand to Reason: Christianity worth thinking about."

Even with the popularity of the so-called "new atheists"—Christopher Hitchens, Daniel Dennett, Richard Dawkins, Sam Harris—it's clear to me that it takes no leap of faith to believe in God. In fact, the more we learn about science, the more *credible* Christianity becomes. That's why the number one philosophical atheist in the world, Antony Flew, did a dramatic about-face and embraced theism—against his will, as it were—on the strength of the scientific evidence for a designer.[2]

Believing in leprechauns is a leap of faith. Believing in God is like believing in atoms. You follow the evidence of what you *can* see to conclude the existence of something you *cannot* see. The process is exactly the same. The effect needs a cause adequate to explain it.

There is nothing unreasonable about the idea of a personal God creating the material universe. A Big Bang needs a "big Banger," it seems to me. A complex set of instructions (as in DNA) needs an author. A blueprint requires an engineer. A moral law needs a moral law giver. This is not a leap. This is a step of intelligent reflection.

It's also not a leap to believe in the Jesus of the Gospels. Eminent historian Will Durant, author of the 11 volume set, *The Story of Civilization*, after a careful assessment of all the evidence, concluded:

> No one reading these scenes can doubt the reality of the figure behind them. That a few simple men should in one genera- tion have invented so powerful and appealing a personality, so lofty an ethic, and so inspiring a vision of human brotherhood, would be a miracle far more incredible than any recorded in the Gospels.

All views and religions give you a picture of the world. That's what a worldview is. The more I read, the more I study, the more I thoughtfully reflect, though, the more I'm convinced that Jesus doesn't just give us a view of the world. He gives us a view of *reality*. When you follow Him, you're not wishing on a star; you're living in the real world.

Thoughtfully,

Greg

Admiration of Your Family, Friends...and *Adversaries?*

A few summers ago, every morning you could find me working at my desk, pounding out text for my book *Tactics: A Game Plan for Discussing Your Christian Convictions.*

It's hard work, writing. I don't particularly like it. Then something comes across my desk that reminds me of why we all labor so hard at STR: a compliment from the other side. I think you'll be encouraged by it as I was.

A very, very left-leaning online magazine wrote this about a secular documentary on abortion featuring Steve Wagner, an STR speaker at the time:

> An instructor [Steve] shows his students footage of a sidewalk debate/shouting match between a rape victim who's had an abortion and two pro-life men.
>
> As the instructor points out what the pro-lifers are doing right and wrong in the debate, we keep waiting for the filmmakers to move in for the kill, to mark this instructor as an object of ridicule. But they never do. The guy is making perfect sense.
>
> He criticizes the two pro-lifers for ganging up on the pro-choice woman, for refusing to show any sympathy for the fact that she was raped, and for being generally loutish. He's an articulate, intelligent, calm presence.

> Suddenly, a chill creeps up your spine: I hope there are people on the pro-choice side who are equally perceptive and balanced.

Admiration from an adversary is the most delicious—and reliable—form of flattery:

> "Articulate, intelligent, calm." "Perceptive and balanced." "The guy is making perfect sense."

Steve's instruction is a lesson of diplomacy in action. It's also a lesson to you and me about how to measure our effectiveness: When even the opposition has to admire the tact and balance of our approach, then we know we're onto something.

There's a reason we get compliments like this, even given grudgingly from those who disagree. We make it our goal to develop the ten intellectual and character virtues listed in the Ambassador's Creed found under "Resources" on our home page at str.org.

Here were three that were in play—and captured on film—during Steve's instruction:

- **Patient.** An Ambassador won't quarrel, but will listen in order to understand, then with gentleness seek to respectfully engage those who disagree.

- **Tactical.** An Ambassador adapts to each unique person and situation, maneuvering with wisdom to challenge bad thinking, presenting the truth in an understandable and compelling way.

- **Attractive.** An Ambassador will act with grace, kindness, and good manners, and will not dishonor Christ in his conduct.

How do you manifest virtues like this under fire? Being winsome and attractive as an ambassador for Christ does not come naturally for me, for Steve, or for anyone else. It's a habit developed on purpose through practice.

That's why every month I reread the Ambassador's Creed. It's on my schedule. If I don't, I forget. I start acting "generally loutish." It's my nature. It's human nature.

So here's a question for you that may be painful to answer, but should be asked frequently: What do your adversaries say about *you*? Your co-workers, your roommates, your relatives— what do they say about *your* character when your back is turned?

Sure, they won't always like your *message*. You can usually count on that. But your *method* should make you stand out from the crowd. It is part of the measure of your success as an ambassador.

I suggest you print out a copy of the Ambassador's Creed and paste it where you can see it every day. If you're like me, you need the reminder.

The nice thing about regular, thoughtful practice is that eventually it builds a habit. And habits define your character.

Warmly,

Greg

Daily Devotion, Rather than Daily Devotions

I know that nourishing our relationship with God is an important part of guarding the treasure entrusted to us. But one way of pursuing that—having a daily "quiet time"—has always been difficult for me. Maybe it's been hard for you, too.

First, I've never done well with the ritual because I could never be consistent. The fact that I'm not really an early morning person combined with a chaotic schedule both seem to sabotage my best intentions.

Second, I don't think you have to have "daily devotions" to be a good Christian. It's become somewhat of an Evangelical sacrament, a source of blessing for many, but also a source of guilt for others who don't (or can't) keep the regimen.

Yes, the Bible says we should pray, study, and meditate—no question there—but it doesn't demand a particular time or pattern. There are a number of ways to satisfy that requirement. Jesus, David, and others often started their days with prayer, but that doesn't mean it's the best pattern for you and me.

Third, I've long suspected the effort is somewhat misdirected. Quiet times are encouraged as a way to "get closer to God," meant to accomplish a subjective goal (generate emotional closeness), not an objective one (gain spiritual understanding).

It's not that such a goal is wrong as much as it's wrong-headed. Feeling close to God, it seems to me, is much like the pursuit of happiness. It's gained not as a goal in itself, but as the outcome of pursuing some other goal. To get something for yourself, you have to focus on something else: God, in this case.

So I have a recommendation. Instead of trying (unsuccessfully) to have devotions every morning, I have *devotion*. That is, I take five to ten minutes early in the day to focus on God—not to get something from Him, but to actively devote myself to Him for the day. After I sing a hymn or two, I use a biblical prayer (I'll share it with you in a moment) as a guide to express my dedication to the Lord.

Devotion (in the sense I'm using the word) is different from "devotions." My goal isn't to squeeze a sense of well-being out of the encounter, but to focus entirely on Him, worshipping Him, thanking Him and devoting myself to His purposes for the day. The focus is entirely on God—not on my feelings—surrendering myself to the Father, no matter how I feel nor what befalls me. It's fairly brief by design, but still very meaningful.

My moments of devotion may develop into a longer prayer time, but they don't have to.

Instead, no matter what my schedule is, I can start each day *devoted* to Christ, then anticipate time for regular prayer and supplication later in the day by scheduling it or squeezing it in using methods I discussed elsewhere (see "10 Tips to Help Your Prayer Life" at str.org).

I suggest using a biblical prayer as a model. Many have used the prayer of Jabez for this purpose. I don't care for this because it's too general and therefore invites abuse, people making the prayer into a kind of talisman or charm (though I don't think that was author Bruce Wilkinson's intent).

Instead, I have used prayers like the prayer of Paul found in Colossians 1:9-12. For a season I prayed this prayer in personalized form almost every day for myself, my wife, and my family. Here's my adaptation:

> I pray that we may be filled with the knowledge of Your will in all spiritual wisdom and understanding, so that we may walk in a manner worthy of You, Lord, to please You in all respects, bearing fruit in every good work and increasing in the knowledge of God; strengthened with all power, according to Your glorious might, for the attaining of all steadfastness and patience; joyously giving thanks to the Father.

I add other personal sentiments before and after, as seems appropriate, but this prayer is the core.

Notice that when you pray this way the focus is entirely on God and His purposes. You ask for knowledge, wisdom, and understanding so you can honor and please God, bearing fruit in your daily walk. You ask for power so you can attain steadfastness and patience. You ask for joy in the context of thanksgiving.

As you can see, it will be very difficult to co-opt this prayer for selfish purposes. But it's perfect to help you and I start our day on the right foot, devoting ourselves to God regardless of how we feel.

If you've been having trouble with "quiet times," try daily *devotion* for two weeks. Write Colossians 1:9-12 on a card and use it as a guide. Gather a small collection of favorite songs—not ones that report your feelings, but ones that focus on the Lord—and use them to begin your devotion.

All good ambassadors need to stay in close contact with their sovereign. This is one small way to help you accomplish that. It may even become a habit. Of course, it's not meant to substitute for times of extended prayer. But it may help you consistently start your day *devoted* to the Lord even when you can't schedule "devotions" first thing.

Devoted to Christ,

Greg

Ban Your God Talk

Tell me if this sounds familiar: "I know you think you understand what you thought I said. What you don't understand is that what you thought I said is not what I meant."

Hugh Hewitt—nationally syndicated talk show host and skilled Christian ambassador—once told me that as Christians we have to reinvent how we talk about God. I think he's right. Too often we're misunderstood. As a result, we've missed some valuable "moments of truth."

For example, on Larry King once an able Christian theologian talked with confidence and polish about his "faith." He was winsome and engaging, explaining his "beliefs" with clarity and confidence. In fact, his beliefs were the same as mine.

So what's the problem?

I don't think the audience understood what he meant. I think they heard his words in an entirely different way than he was using them. If I said, "Abraham Lincoln was the 16th president of the United States," people would know I was talking about history.

By contrast, if I said, "I believe in the resurrection of Jesus" (as the theologian did), most people would not think I was talking about historical facts, but personal faith: my sentiments, my feelings, my preferences.

From their perspective, words like "faith" and "belief" don't describe the *world*, they describe *me*. Statements about Jesus may reflect *personal* "truths" (i.e., "true for me"). But they're not really true; they are not facts. They are merely "beliefs"—well-intentioned falsehoods, useful fictions, convenient illusions.

That's not what we *say*. It's what they *hear*.

I notice the same thing whenever a newspaper recounts the rescue of a hiker who, against all odds, survives a deadly blizzard. "My faith got me through the ordeal," the hiker says.

The article concludes, "His strong faith saved him." In other words, it was the strength of the hiker's *belief*, not the strength of the One *in whom* he believed that secured his survival. That's probably not what the hiker meant, but it's what the reporter heard.

Let me suggest a simple adjustment. Since there's often a difference between what we say and what others hear, don't give them the chance to misunderstand. Instead of using emotive "faith" language, use the language of truth.

Don't talk about your faith; talk about what you think is true. Don't talk about your beliefs; talk about your convictions, about what you've been convinced of. Don't talk about your personal values; talk about what is actually right and wrong.

Don't just think about what *you mean*; think about what *others hear*.

The question "Do you take the Gospels literally?" is also loaded. A simple "yes" could be misleading, so I answer in a way that makes my own meaning clear: "I think the Bible accurately records what actually happened." No ambiguity there.

I've actually encouraged Christians to ban words like "faith" and "belief" from their vocabulary because these words no longer communicate what we intend them to.

It's not that faith isn't valuable. It's vital. But faith is often misunderstood as a "leap," a blind, desperate lunge into the darkness. It sounds too much like religious wishful thinking.

The STR Ambassador's Creed says that an Ambassador is "reasonable." He has informed convictions, not just feelings or religious sentiments. When he talks about Jesus, he is careful to communicate that he is talking about facts, not just the a kind of religious wishful thinking that words like "faith" and "belief" frequently conjure up.

So for me, instead of using "faith" language, I say, "Here are the facts, as I see them." I use the language of truth during my moments of truth. I think you should, too.

Standing firm in the facts,

Greg

A Lesson in Character

I learned an important lesson once while doing a debate on relativism at the University of Washington in Seattle.

My opponent was Clive, an M.A. Philosophy grad and former punk-rocker who worked on campus as a residence director. He was steeped in postmodernism. He was also an atheist.

I always go into debates a little nervous, and this was no exception. Sure, I'm confident in my material. In addition, I always play it safe by defending a very modest claim, in this case that some universal moral principles actually exist.

As it turns out, this is very hard for people to deny. Arguing there are objective moral truths is entirely reasonable, in spite of the fact that there appear to be so many objectors. In fact, it's becoming hard to find anyone with advanced credentials who is willing to take the other side anymore.

For one, there are too many obvious counter-examples. The debate is over when one claims—as the relativist must—that there are no objective moral differences between the rapes, tortures, and murders of an Uday and Qusay

Hussein, on the one hand, and the kindness, self-sacrifice, and deep humanity of a Mother Teresa and Martin Luther King on the other.

Even so, I've learned not to be overly confident.

My nervousness is natural from a human perspective (yes, even I get butterflies). It's also helpful, in a way. I don't want to go into a situation cocky and over-confident. I could get humbled. A haughty spirit often precedes a stumbling, Solomon warns (Prov. 16:18). Plus, postmoderns are especially sensitive to smugness. They pick up on it immediately and are understandably put off.

Sometimes it helps when I remind myself that my opponent is nervous, too, often even more than I am. This was the case in Seattle. Clive had never debated before and expressed dismay to my host, Duane of Campus Crusade for Christ, when he saw my own credentials.

Of course, when I learned this I relaxed a bit, sensing my advantage. Duane, however, saw an advantage of a different kind.

"Let's do everything we can to put Clive at ease," he told me the day of the debate. "I want him and the audience to see that we're not just smart, we're gracious, too. We care about him as much as we care about the argument. So I've arranged for the three of us to have dinner together before the event."

Immediately my anxiety skyrocketed. "Are you out of your mind?" I thought to myself. Why simply surrender my psychological advantage?

I didn't reveal my shallow thinking, though.

"Sure," I nodded. "Sounds fine to me."

We dined at a local greasy spoon and mused about theology and philosophy over hotdogs and cokes. As we talked, I saw a fellow human being who needed the truth, not an opponent who needed to be beaten.

I even coached Clive on debate techniques he might consider, and assured him this would be an amicable discussion about ideas and not a full-tilt battle. He was noticeably relieved.

The debate went smoothly for me. Regarding the facts, it was obviously one-sided. But because of our time over dinner, it was easy for me to be relaxed, even-handed, and charitable, though I was free to be aggressive in my critique.

After the debate was over Clive shook my hand. "Thank you," he whispered, "for handling me with kid-gloves and not destroying me, as I know you could have." He knew he had been bested, but not beaten.

In situations like these I always try to apply one of STR's guiding values: All human beings are made in the image of God and are therefore valuable ends in themselves, not just instrumental means to other ends that are valuable. Yet in this debate Duane had helped me to "excel still more." I was deeply instructed by his example, and it profoundly affected my ability to be a better ambassador in the future.

I thought of Paul's charitable posture when reasoning with Agrippa in Acts 22, an attitude he explained in 2 Timothy 2:24-25. "And the Lord's bond-servant must not be quarrelsome, but be kind to all…patient when wronged, with gentleness correcting those who are in opposition, if perhaps God may grant them repentance leading to the knowledge of the truth."

This is exactly what Duane had in mind, of course. Clive, the audience, and the Kingdom were all better served because of his wisdom.

For the Kingdom,

Greg

Why an Atheist Considered Christianity

How do you reach out to someone who is not looking for God and does not even believe He exists? That's a question I've asked myself more than once, which is why the opening lines of one particular little book immediately grabbed my attention:

> This book sets out to do what might seem to be a straight-forward task: to recount the experiences of a few months in my life in which I walked away from atheism and entered into Christian faith.

Nothing is ever as simple as that. It is no light matter to meet God after having denied Him all one's life.

A delightful read—and also a fascinating radio interview—followed. The book, *Not God's Type: A Rational Academic Finds a Radical Faith*, is a memoir by Holly Ordway of her journey from atheism to Christ.

The guide God used to shepherd Holly on her pilgrimage was not a professional apologist, but rather her fencing coach—an ordinary, thoughtful Christian named Josh who lived out his love for Jesus for an entire year with Holly before the name "Jesus" ever came up in their conversation.

Josh was the personification of the second critical characteristic of a good ambassador: wisdom, "an artful method." Here are some of the lessons I gleaned from Holly's account of her friendship with Josh and his wife, Heidi.

One, respect people. Period. Treat others as special in God's eyes regardless of their spiritual condition. To Josh, Holly wasn't a heathen to be converted, but a human to be valued. He never reproached her for her unbelief, but treated her with genuine grace, dignity, and honor. He also did not fulfill any of the negative stereotypes she had of Christians. Instead, his character silently spoke volumes.

Two, begin at *their* beginning. Start at square one *for that person*. The basic message of forgiveness rests upon a number of assumptions about God, morality, guilt, Jesus, and more. Don't presume the other person has crossed all those bridges.

"What's helpful varies from person to person," Holly pointed out. "I was glad for Josh's willingness to be a guide as I entered this strange new territory, rather than trying to choose the path for me." Like Josh, be a coach, a guide for the journey. Don't choose the path for them. Answer *their* questions first, not the questions you think they should be asking.

Three, don't push. "Josh didn't try to close the deal on me—ever," Holly wrote. If he had, she would have bolted. "Pressing for a decision [too early] would have been a disaster. It would have taken very little to make me close up and turn away, vulnerable and confused as I was."

Don't be afraid to move slowly. People need time to think, to digest, to reflect before they can ultimately commit. Don't press for a "decision" for Christ when a conversion to Christ is what's necessary. Trust the Spirit to do the deep work. Remember, God is in control.

Four, use questions. Josh consistently used carefully crafted questions to make his point. "If you could do something wrong that would benefit yourself," he asked, "and you knew that no one would ever know about it, would you do it?" When Holly said no, he asked, "Why not? If there is no God, why be moral when it would benefit you personally to be immoral?" Josh was not trying to score points in an argument. Instead, he was probing the tension in Holly's worldview, graciously challenging her inconsistency while presenting new ideas for her to consider.

Five, be clear. Make the central issues unmistakable. When Holly asked Josh what would happen to her when she died, he told her the truth—simply, without ambiguity, but without animosity. "I believe we will come before God in judgment," he said, "and He will give each person either *perfect justice* or *perfect mercy*."

When asked, "What, exactly, would I be getting myself into?," Josh told her two things that Jesus said: "My yoke is light," and "Take up your cross and follow Me." "I'll let you ponder that." Josh did not shy away from the fact that mercy and safety could be found only under His cross.

Josh was especially deft at navigating the challenge that Holly's situation presented. Sensitivity like his is developed over time, learning how to proceed with wisdom—"an artful method"—based on knowledge—"an accurately informed mind."

Standing with you for the Gospel,

Greg

Why It's Sometimes Smart to Agree with an Atheist

I want to let you in on a little epiphany, a moment of revelation I had while prepping for my national radio debate with atheist and *Skeptic* magazine founder, Michael Shermer.[3]

Here's the "inspired" insight: Sometimes it's better to move *towards* an objection rather than *away* from it, to *embrace* a charge rather than *run* from it.

I was first exposed to this maneuver in a movie. In the opening scenes of "Clear and Present Danger," a man with connections to the president was found dead in what appeared to be a drug deal gone bad. To contain the PR damage, the president's advisors suggested he immediately downplay the relationship and distance himself from the problem.

Analyst Jack Ryan (played by Harrison Ford) suggested just the opposite. "If they ask if you were friends," he counseled, "say, 'No, he was a *good* friend.' If they ask if he was a good friend, say 'We were *lifelong* friends.' It would give them no place to go. Nothing to report. No story."

In other words, don't run from the problem;

run *towards* it and defuse it. Don't evade; invade. Embrace it, undermine its relevance, and take the wind out of its sails.

In certain situations we face, that's good advice. For example, I fully expected Shermer to fire off the atheist's standard response to evidence for intelligent design: "If you argue for ID, then you're going to have to deal with the problem of imperfect design." In other words, if God designed living organisms, their design would be perfect. Clearly there are flaws, however. Therefore, there was no designer.

If that point came up, I planned to follow Ryan's recommendation. I'd say "Michael, you're absolutely right. If I'm going to argue for an intelligent designer, then I *am* going to have to deal with that problem. But you're not going to get off the hook that easily. One anomaly doesn't nullify the overwhelming evidence for design. That would be like denying a wristwatch was designed because it ran three minutes slow. You're straining at a gnat, but swallowing a camel."

This challenge to ID isn't really an argument against the evidence for design. It's a *distraction* from that evidence. By moving *toward* the challenge, I'd blunt the objection by telegraphing to the radio audience I was aware of the difficulty and wasn't shaken by it. Shermer would have "no place to go. Nothing to report. No story."

As it turned out, that issue didn't come up, but something like it did. Shermer pointed out that if the Bible is a guide to morality, then I'd have to pick and choose which biblical commands to embrace. My response: "You're absolutely right, Michael."

Yes, I explained, I *would* have to do the hard work of sorting the rules out. But that's true of every ethical system, even his. I faced no bigger challenge than he did with his "objective" evolutionary morality. I agreed with the problem, then denied its significance.

I've heard Christians stumped when atheists charged, "There are lots of gods *you* don't believe in, too: Zeus, Jupiter, Thor, etc. We atheists just believe in one *less* god than you."

It turns out the atheist is exactly right on this point, but it does him no good. Believing in one less god than a theist is exactly what distinguishes atheists from monotheists. Nothing meaningful follows from this observation. The flummoxed Christian could have simply said, "Yes, you're right. You do. You believe in one less God than I do. Bachelors also have one less wife than married men. What's your point?" Then watch the challenge fizzle.

In the future, I plan to take this tack more often. Maybe it would be a good move for you, too. The objector says, "This is a problem," and instead of backpedaling, we move towards it and embrace it. "Yes," we admit, "that is an issue, but it's not ultimately relevant, decisive, or damaging when you see it in perspective and consider the evidence."

When a naysayer raises an objection, it is meant to push us off balance and put us on the ropes in a defensive position. In some cases, stepping forward instead of backwards changes that dynamic and the objection goes dead in the water.

Because of His grace,

Greg

Bloom Where You're Planted

My wife had a plaque hanging in our kitchen that offered sage advice for times of waiting. It simply said, "Bloom where you're planted."

I tell you this for two reasons.

First, in 1985 I gave a sermon called "I Hate to Wait" based on the life of Joseph. As personal background to the talk, I shared my intense frustration with being in God's "waiting room" for years in the area of career ministry.

I'd participated in three summer outreach projects, was a missionary overseas twice (Eastern Europe in '76, and Thailand in '82), and gave countless talks and sermons as a guest speaker around Southern California. I was ready—or so I thought. Yet as hard as I tried, I never seemed to be able to find my niche in a full-time position. I was the perpetual "trainee."

The second reason I tell you about my wife's plaque is because of how STR got started. On May 1, 1993, fifty faithful friends and prayer partners gathered with me in the Ocean View room at Hope Chapel in Hermosa Beach, California, to hear a bold concept I called "Stand to Reason."

I challenged them to consider the possibility of what God might do through a small group of people committed to an outrageous idea: an organization dedicated to clear-thinking Christianity.

I asked them each two questions. First, what did they think of this idea? Second, how much would they commit financially that day to help this idea take root?

The individual responses of excitement and personal generosity were overwhelming. Because of the kindness and vision of those fifty people on that birth day of Stand to Reason, we stepped out in faith with an initial $14,800 in commitments of support.

We immediately began selling audiotapes on critical issues confronting Christians. By the following February we had submitted our first three STR tapes for mass production: "Hell Yes: The Terrifying Truth," "The Heathen and the Unknown God," and "The Bible and Homosexuality: Setting the Record Straight."

At our one-year anniversary, May 1994, I commented in a letter to our donors how we had grown from mailing out 55 radio commentaries in January to 661 in April. At our ten year mark our monthly total was 60,000 and climbing.

Which brings me back to the plaque hanging in our kitchen. In the midst of my "waiting room" frustration I coped by following a simple rule: "Bloom where you're planted," a more colloquial way of stating Peter's advice in 1 Peter 4:10-11:

As each one has received a special gift, employ it in serving one another, as good stewards of the manifold grace of God.

Whoever speaks let him speak, as it were, the utterances of God. Whoever serves let him do so as by the strength that God supplies, so that in all things God may be glorified through Jesus Christ.

In all those years of anxious waiting all I could do was pay close attention to what God had given me on any given day, being "faithful with a few things" (Matthew 25:23). Little did I know what was on the horizon.

My advice to you when you're in God's waiting room? Simple. Bloom where you're planted. Look for any opportunity to use your gifts. Be faithful in serving. Trust God to use your efforts for His Kingdom. Then watch God work.

For the Kingdom,

Greg

New Movement of the Spirit? So What?

Over a decade ago, I offered a simple piece of advice meant to protect Christians from ever being taken in by any religious fad, novel teaching, or alleged new manifestation of the Spirit.

At that time, a movement variously called the "Toronto Blessing," the "Laughing Revival," and the "Brownsville Revival" stirred up contention for the bizarre behavior associated with it.

Years later, Todd Bentley of Fresh Fire Ministries in Lakeland, Florida, grabbed Christian headlines with what some have called the "Lakeland Revival." His style and methods were controversial for the same kinds of reasons "Toronto" was.

Circumstances like these give thoughtful Christians pause. On the one hand, when spiritual manifestations seem bizarre, the urge is strong to run the other way. On the other hand, the Scriptures themselves record God's unusual activity in the past. Aslan is not a tame lion, after all. No sincere Christian wants to resist the Holy Spirit and offend God.

My advice with Lakeland was the same as

with Toronto and any other unusual "new movement" of the Spirit that pops up in the future:
You can safely ignore it.

I gleaned this advice from Second Timothy,
Paul's swan song, his final thoughts before fac-
ing the executioner. In it, he passes the torch
of the Gospel to Timothy with a sober warning:
Difficult times are coming.

First, there will be trouble in the world:

But realize this, that in the last days difficult times will come.
For men will be lovers of self, lovers of money, boastful, ar-
rogant, revilers, disobedient to parents, ungrateful, unholy,
unloving, irreconcilable, malicious gossips, without self-control,
brutal, haters of good, treacherous, reckless, conceited, lovers
of pleasure rather than lovers of God (2 Tim 3:1-4).

Second, there will be trouble in the church:

For the time will come when they will not endure sound
doctrine; but wanting to have their ears tickled, they will ac-
cumulate for themselves teachers in accordance to their own
desires; and will turn away their ears from the truth, and will
turn aside to myths (2 Tim. 4:3-4).

Trouble is on the horizon, Paul says—trouble
in the world, and trouble in the church. He then
gives Timothy the antidote, a solution found in
three simple words: "You, however, continue...."

You, however, continue in the things you have learned and
become convinced of, knowing from whom you have learned
them....All Scripture is inspired by God and profitable for teaching, for reproof, for correction, for training in righteousness;
that the man of God may be adequate, equipped for every good
work (2 Tim 3:14-4:2).

In Paul's final warning to the church, he does
not counsel Timothy to face the challenges of
the future by embracing new movements of
the Spirit. Instead, he tells him to look backwards, to continue in and guard what has al-

ready been revealed.

This is Paul's message throughout his entire letter. "Retain the standard of sound words which you *have heard* from me" (1:13). "Guard... the treasure which *has been* entrusted to you" (1:14). "And the things which you *have heard* from me...these entrust to faithful men, who will be able to teach others also" (2:2).

Paul warns of a time of moral chaos falling on the world and theological chaos falling on the church. The antidote for both is the same: Steady at the helm. Guard what has already been entrusted to you. Continue in the things which you have already learned.

Everything we need to be fruitful and productive, to be trained in righteousness, to be adequately equipped for every good work, has already been revealed. For Paul, all the *old* stuff was all the *right* stuff.

New movement of the Spirit? Maybe. And maybe not. I don't have to decide. Instead, I'm taking the safe route by heeding Paul's advice and focusing on the *old* movement of the Spirit. And so should you.

In His service,

Greg

Equipped to Engage

Sometimes it's the little things that have the greatest impact on others for Christ. Usually the best entry into a conversation, or the most effective response to a challenge, is the uncomplicated one. Having handy responses ready for the right moment is a big part of what it means to be equipped to engage.

For example, a Christian brother named Jim was in the habit of visiting a WW2 veteran every few months. His "How ya doin'?" was usually met with a polite "Doin' just fine."

One time, though, Jim took it a step further, having resolved to make more of the opportunities God gave him each day. "How are you doing *spiritually*?" he added the next time they met.

The question caught the old vet with his guard down. He attempted a reply, but his words trailed off into silence. With God, apparently, he wasn't "Doin' just fine." Jim now had an opening, and gently shared the love of Christ with his elderly friend.

Sometimes something as simple as "Can I pray for you" can have a dramatic effect. When you're talking with someone and there seems to be any sadness, frustration, or distress, make the offer. Then pray right there, simply, directly…and briefly.

Don't be surprised if your friend is choked up when you finish. This is a very powerful way to show you care and to demonstrate that knowing Christ is practical and personal.

There are other times someone dishes out a stock retort meant to stonewall you. The right short response can completely turn the tables.

Once in a restaurant in Seattle a waitress told me "All religions are basically the same," expecting that would end the conversation in her favor. I simply asked, "Oh? In what way?"

Those four simple words stopped her in her tracks. Her long silence convinced me she had no idea how to answer. She obviously had never looked closely at other religions. If she had, she'd have known they were worlds apart.

Here's another example. Sometimes it's difficult to know how to respond when someone says, "Who's to say?" It occurred to me last night while stranded in L.A. traffic that there's a very simple response: The one who has *the best reasons*, that's who's to say. That's the way truth always works. A claim is only as strong as the reasons behind it.

As a general rule, using simple, leading questions is an almost effortless way to introduce spiritual topics to a conversation without seeming abrupt. At STR we call this the Columbo tactic, named after the bumbling and seemingly inept TV detective whose remarkable success was based on an innocent query: "Do you mind if I ask you a question?"

Columbo is most powerful if you have a plan of attack. Generally when I ask a question I have a goal in mind. I'm alerted to some weakness, flaw, or contradiction in another's view that I want to expose in a disarming way.

Other times the question is an open-ended "What do you mean by that?" delivered in a mild, genuinely inquisitive fashion. The general topic can be anything broadly related to spiritual things. Next, begin to probe with questions, gently guiding the conversation in what you think might be a spiritually productive direction.

The follow-up question, "How did you come to that conclusion?," graciously assumes the non-Christian has reasons for her view and is not just emoting. It gives her a chance to express her rationale (if she has one), giving you more material to work with.

Occasionally someone will quip, "I don't have any reasons. I just believe it." To which I ask, "Why would you believe something when you have no reason to think it's true?" This is a genuine—and very appropriate—question. And it's simple.

While on vacation one year in Wisconsin, I noticed that the woman helping us at the 1-hour photo was wearing a large pentagram—a 5-pointed star generally associated with the occult—around her neck.

"Does that have religious significance," I asked, "or is it just jewelry?"

"It has religious significance," she answered. "The five points stand for earth, wind, fire, water, and spirit. I'm a pagan."

My wife, unaware that "pagan" referred to Wicca (witchcraft) and earth worship, laughed in amazement at what seemed like a remarkably candid confession. "I've never heard anyone actually admit right out they were pagan," she explained.

"It's an earth religion," the woman at the counter explained, "like the Native Americans."

"So you're Wiccan?" I continued. She nodded. This led to a fascinating conversation made possible by a very simple thing: a question about something she wore.

Always be alert to the little things. Don't take an elaborate route when a simple one will do just fine. It's an important part of being equipped to engage.

Your partner for truth,

Greg

Seasons of Dryness

Seasons of dryness are part of our walk with Christ. They are a natural element in the ebb and flow of any healthy relationship. Sometimes our spiritual gardens burst with life. Other times they're parched, dry, and brown.

Cultivating sensible faith requires recognition and attention to these seasons so we don't dry up. For followers of Christ, a vital element of that cultivation is prayer.

I have to confess, prayer has never come easy for me. For a few hardy prayer warriors, talking with God is as easy as breathing; it happens almost effortlessly for them. When you ask them how they do it, they simply shrug and reply, "I just pray."

Unfortunately, for some of us that's about as helpful as Babe Ruth saying "I just hit the ball." We need a little more instruction to get the job done.

Most of those whose prayers are recorded in the Bible engaged both their hearts and their minds in the process. We should do the same.

I try to start my prayer time with a hymn that moves my heart because it expresses my genuine wonder or affection towards God, or my humble surrender to Him. Then I spend time thanking God for specific things in my life. Finally, I focus on petition, praying intelligently, specifically, and persuasively.

Here are some other practical guidelines I've personally found helpful in cultivating a more fruitful prayer life. If you begin incorporating a few of them, I'm confident your own time with the Lord will improve and your faith will be refreshed.

- **Make a list** of prayer items on a scratch pad to guide you.

- **Choose a specific place** to pray away from distractions so you can concentrate. Ringing phones and crying children will sabotage your time before it gets started.

- **Pray out loud**. Many people can pray under their breath or in their minds for long periods and still maintain focus and intensity, but for most of us it's a quick ticket to dreamland. When we pray out loud we have to form intelligent sentences. We have to concentrate on what we're praying about.

- **Keep a note pad handy** so you can jot down things that come to mind while you're before the Lord. Sometimes you'll get great ideas totally unrelated to what you've been praying about. If you jot them down, you can quickly get back to the topic at hand without being too distracted.

- **Pray short, sincere prayers.** If the thought of laboring over a topic wears you out, pray in short paragraphs instead. A few sentences may be all that's needed to exhaust the topic for you for the time being. If so, just move on to the next item without feeling guilty for your brevity. The prayer Jesus taught His disciples contained a series of short requests.

- **Redeem time for prayer** from unused corners of your schedule. When driving, talk to the Lord instead of screaming at traffic. Busy homemakers can combine prayer with housework, especially if the task doesn't require a lot of concentration. Joggers and cyclists can use their workout time for prayer. Sometimes my most satisfying and intimate conversations with the Lord have been during long walks.

- **Pray with someone else.** Though some prayers can only be said in solitude, there will be times you'll want to join hearts with another person in prayer. If you commit to meet on a regular basis, the accountability can help build consistency. Such prayer trysts often become powerful, life-changing habits.

- **Keep a prayer journal.** This can be done easily with a computer. Here are two variations of this idea. The first is to keep track of what you prayed for and when you prayed for it. Leave a space to jot down the answer when it comes. This will help you to keep alert to God's answer so you can thank Him promptly. Sometimes prayer answers come in the back door and you don't want them to slip by you. The second variation is to write the entire prayer in your journal. Make it a personal letter to the Lord.

Try out some of these ideas. They can make a

big difference, bringing refreshment during the
inevitable dry spells.

In His grip,

Greg

Have You Been Accused of Being Closed-Minded?

My niece, Kirsten, has a friend named Aiman who accused her of being closed-minded simply because she believed Jesus' claim that He was the only way of salvation. If you have encountered this yourself, you might be interested in what I told her.

Notice that the complaint here is not that Kirsten was wrong about Jesus. Aiman conveniently side-stepped that issue. Instead, she was wrong—"closed-minded"—simply for thinking she was right. Apparently Aiman was not aware that he cannot refute a view by attacking something else—in this case Kirsten's character.

First, it is completely proper to think that if your view is true, opposing views must be mistaken. How could it be different? For example, if it is true that all religions lead to God, then it is false that only one religion leads to God. It is nonsense to affirm that there are both many ways to God and that there is only one way to God.

I think you can see very quickly that regardless of whoever is correct on the theological point, the other person must be mistaken. Both people must be "narrow" at this juncture. There is no way of escaping it without sounding silly. This is elementary.

In fact, this observation is so basic it would be trivial if it were not that so many people seem to miss it. Ironically, Aiman affirms as much. He thinks himself correct on his pluralism and faults Kirsten for her opposing view. Nothing odd here except, perhaps, that he doesn't consider himself equally closed-minded for doing the same as she.

This leads to a second point. "Narrow-mindedness" is not a proper criticism of *what* you believe, but of *how* you believe it. Here's what I mean.

"Narrow" is the proper and unavoidable way to describe the *content* of just about any belief (as I've just pointed out). "Narrow-minded," however, is entirely different. It refers not to the belief, but to the *person* who won't consider opposing views. Instead, out of dogmatism, bias, or bigotry, he dismisses them without giving them a hearing.

Christians have certainly been guilty of this in the past, but they have no corner on the market. So-called skeptics are frequently narrow-minded in this regard.

Which brings me to my final point. I don't mean to be unkind, but it strikes me that Aiman is (ironically) the closed-minded person in this conversation. He dismisses Kirsten's view as narrow—which, of course, it must be if it is a view at all—without engaging her *reasons* why it might be true. A personal attack ("You're narrow-minded") substitutes for engaging the ideas.

This is classic closed-mindedness.

The way to demonstrate that people like Aiman are making this error is to simply ask them (Columbo style) if *they* are open-minded: Yes or no? Are they genuinely open to the possibility that Jesus is who He claimed to be?

If their openness is authentic, they should be willing to consider Jesus' claim and why He made it. Then they would be in a better position to judge the view itself instead of judging the Christian who holds it.

On his present course, though, Aiman could never admit that. If he were truly open-minded to the possibility Jesus was right, he would be perilously close to becoming the kind of person *he* thinks is closed-minded.

Aiman has boxed himself in. He is not able to escape this self-refuting circle. Based on his definition of openness, he is either not open to even consider Kirsten's view—making him truly closed-minded—or he would have to admit her "narrow" view might be correct—making him just as closed-minded (in his use of the word) as he says she is.

As you can see, Aiman's effort commits suicide, demonstrating that his entire approach is a dead-end. He would be better off abandoning this silly challenge and being open-minded enough to give the Christian view a fair hearing instead of dismissing it.

Barnhouse is alleged to have said that the purpose of an open mind is like the purpose of an open mouth. Eventually it should close down on something solid.

Minds, like mouths, should not be continually gaping open. Sooner or later we have to commit ourselves to some beliefs that seem reasonable. Put another way, we don't want to have our minds so open that our brains fall out.

Thoughtfully open-minded,

Greg

I Held My Tongue and Waited (for Once)

Sometimes conversations with people who differ with us can get awkward. Maybe you don't have the freedom to express your beliefs as freely as you'd like. Maybe the person you're engaging with is more interested in talking than listening.

In those situations, I have a suggestion that could make your job easier: Get back to basics. First, ask questions and listen, a lot. Second, don't swing for the fences. Instead, just try to get on base. Try to make one good point stick.

Let me give you an example of how that basic approach worked for me on a 47-minute flight from Los Angeles to San Jose. I'd settled in for the short hop expecting to get some work done when a middle-aged gentleman sat down next to me.

Stuart, a world-traveling frequent-flier, was in an expansive mood and clearly wanted to talk. He had strong opinions about religion, ideas he advanced without invitation and without reservation. I tossed up a quick "Lord, help me" prayer. Then I listened. And watched. And waited for an opportunity.

We talked the whole flight. Or I should say, Stuart talked the whole flight. I listened, mostly, because Stuart had a lot to say. His extensive travels and survey of world religions had convinced him that, in spite of his Catholic upbringing, the teaching of every religion ultimately boiled down to the same thing. The common core? Love—peaceful coexistence, people getting along.

By contrast, those folks who thought their *own* religion was the right one, they were the problem. The word "hate" slipped in at this point, along with the word "racket," describing religion's passion for passing the hat.

My three-word prayer went off again in my mind. But still I listened. Every sentence I heard contained details I disagreed with, but simply contradicting Stuart wouldn't have helped, so I held my tongue and waited.

I did express concern he might have missed the main point of these different religions, and I mentioned that the existence of racketeers in religion doesn't make all religion a racket (he agreed). Other than that, I said almost nothing. I let him talk.

Eventually Stuart asked what religion I was and I said Christian. He grunted, "So you're saying 90% of the people in the world are wrong and going to Hell?"

"Well, I didn't *say* that," I responded, carefully choosing my own battlefield. "I just don't think they can *all* be right."

Unruffled, Stuart glanced sideways at me and smiled. He was clearly impressed with his own musings. "So, do you think I've done a good job thinking this through?"

"Well, since you asked...no, I don't think you have, Stuart." A startled look replaced his smile, but he didn't get angry because I was answering him, not attacking him.

"I certainly don't say that with any animosity," I continued, "and you *have* done a lot of *thinking* about it. But no, I don't think you've thought through this issue *well*.

"For example, you've considered what seem like similarities in religion, right?" I shrugged. "Look, when you think about it, Islam is not about love, but submission. Christianity is not about love, but forgiveness. Buddhism is not about love, but escaping suffering. Hinduism is not about love, but escaping the illusion of the world. Love may be *significant* in each, but it's not the *central message* of each.

"And what of the differences? Why think a modest similarity is more important than the massive differences?"

I paused as he absorbed the point. "As to your comment about 90% being wrong, I don't see how anyone can avoid that, no matter how much love they have for people. Look, maybe *my* religion is mistaken. Maybe they're *all* wrong. But even if one group gets it right—pick any one, it doesn't matter which—that means all the rest, 75 to 90% of the people on the planet, got it wrong. It's not hate; it's just simple math."

When we landed in San Jose, our chat came to a friendly close. I shook Stuart's hand, wished him all the best, and then quietly entrusted him to God.

Two things stood out for me about this encounter that I don't want you to miss.

First, I waited a long time before jumping in with both feet. Instead of sounding off the first time I heard something I disagreed with, I waited for the right moment. When I wasn't sure of the best way to maneuver, I chose silence and attentive listening.

Second, when my opportunity arrived I was genial, but direct, giving Stuart one main thing to think about, one "stone in his shoe." I wanted him to see that it just didn't add up to say all religions were true. We can all be wrong, but we can't all be right.

So here's my advice. When you're afraid a conversation may get awkward, first, shoot up a quick prayer for help. Then, be patient. Listen, a lot. Ask plenty of questions. Wait for the right opportunity before weighing in. Second, take what God gives you, even if it's less than you hoped for. Don't swing for the stands. Just try to get on base. Make one good point.

It's not really that tricky. It just takes getting back to basics.

Warmly,

Greg

Assessing Your Character

I'm constantly going through the process of assessment. It's become a habit for me. How did I do? Where were my missteps? How can I improve? This is where STR's "Knowledge, Wisdom, and Character" model really comes in handy. It gives me categories to focus on.

Assessing whether I had an accurately informed mind (Knowledge) or an artful method (Wisdom) is the easiest thing to do. To assess the Character element, though—an attractive manner—I need some help.

The hardest part of our personal growth in character is identifying our own flaws, principally because we're not in a good position to observe them. Those close to us, however, are. They see things we'll never notice. The smart thing to do is to enlist them as allies, but this takes a certain amount of courage.

I'd like to offer you a challenge I guarantee will transform your life if you take me up on it. Here it is. Talk to the people closest to you. This will include those who have been with you when sharing your faith, but should also involve those who are around you on a regular basis: family, friends, and business associates. Tell them you're serious about developing your character as an effective ambassador for Christ. Then tell them you need their help.

Invite them to give you feedback on the way you come across to others. Ask each to tell you specifically how he thinks you can improve. Have them focus on behaviors, not intangibles (e.g., if they say you're too aggressive, ask for the specific conduct that appears that way to them). If you have a lot to work on, you may want to protect yourself from being overwhelmed by asking each person to suggest just one thing for the time being that stands out that they think you need to address.

There are three important rules to keep in mind about this exercise.

First, you have to resist the impulse to defend yourself. You can do this best by simply keeping silent, only speaking to ask clarifying questions. Take notes if you need to. In fact, I recommend it.

Second, you must make it clear you won't retaliate, even subtly, for what's been shared. If anyone fears being candid with you, they won't be much help. The key here is to get their insight on how you can improve. They're in the best position to give it, but must feel safe before they'll be honest with you.

Third, thank them. It's not easy for people to give feedback like that, but my personal life has been transformed by this practice.

I regularly solicit input from my wife, my staff, and those who I'm mentoring. Then I listen carefully to what they have to say. Sometimes criticism comes unsolicited from a member of the audience. Nonetheless, I still try to pay attention to it, even if the person is obviously hostile. I listen carefully and thank him for his suggestions.

Once you've gathered the information, get somewhere by yourself and do these four things.

First, have a good cry if you need it, then pray for grace, strength, and wisdom to make the best use out of what you've been told.

Next, analyze the feedback. Keep in mind that some people may have missed the mark in their suggestions. However, if the same thing comes up more than once, that's a good indication others are on to something. Don't ignore it, shrug it off, or try to explain it away. That will do you no good.

Finally, outline your plans for change and "publish" it, that is, make your intentions clear about the specific actions you'll be changing. This helps you to stay accountable.

In addition to giving you valuable information on what you need to work on, this habit produces another benefit. You will be *modeling* character because you will be working on two virtues—courage and humility—just by doing the exercise. This is bound to have a salutary effect on your friends, associates, and especially your family. They will see your vulnerability and personal progress as you apply what you learn in future opportunities.

In His grip,

The Power of One
Simple Word

I would like to tip you off to the power of a simple two-letter word.

When used properly, it has the ability to stop an aggressive challenger in his tracks, turn the tables, and get him thinking. This modest word is a little giant, putting the ball back into the other person's court and putting you in the driver's seat of an otherwise out-of-control conversation.

That word, used as a question, is "So?" Here is why—and how—it works.

Many challenges to your convictions as a follower of Christ amount to nothing more than "trash talk," cleverly worded insults meant to intimidate, denigrate, disparage, and subdue. They have great rhetorical power and initially sound completely persuasive.

The problem is, trash talk is just that—trash, a garbage attack that has no bearing on the issue at hand. You need a reply that will immediately show it for the nonsense it is.

Often, your best response to trash talk is to simply agree with the put-down and then use that powerful, two-letter word. "So?" Basically you're asking, "Even if the charge were true, what follows from it?"

Here's one example: "Christians are stupid." The afternoon before I lectured to a crowd of 400 students at UC San Diego, I learned that many of the young people on campus thought Christians were stupid. That information gave me a good opening for my talk.

"I understand that many of you think Christians are stupid. Well," I admitted, "many of them are. So? Many non-Christians are stupid too, so I don't know what that gets you. Tonight I'm here to explain why Christianity is not stupid."

Do you see how the air goes out of the Christians-are-stupid dig once it's exposed as trash talk? Religious people of all stripes can be gullible, irrational, easily misled, and emotionally manipulated. So what? They are no different from the rest of the population. A critic is going to have to come up with something more substantial to discredit Christianity.

Here's another: "Christians are hypocrites." I always have this simple response ready for that barb: "Yep, many are. So?" Some Christians may be hypocrites—fakers. Church-goers can be self-centered, judgmental, gossipy louts. It's tragic, but what does that tell you about God, Jesus, or Christianity? Nothing.

And then there's the classic: "God is a crutch." With that charge I wholeheartedly agree. God is a crutch. So? Crippled people need crutches. For multitudes, God has been an "ever present help in time of trouble." How could that possibly be an argument *against* God?

Let me give you a tip. Whenever someone faults an idea by attacking something about the *person* who holds the idea rather than giving evidence against the *idea* itself, you know he's talking trash. Ridicule is not an argument. Making disparaging observations about someone's psychology is not evidence. Finding vices with religious people tells you nothing about God or religion.

Here's why this is a losing strategy if you care about truth: You cannot refute a view by attacking something else. These rhetorical tricks may be compelling to the untutored who can't see through them, but they're nothing more than trash.

And the simple word "So?" shows it to be so.

In His service,

Greg

The Little Things that Count

How does it look to be an ambassador for Christ in the nuts and bolts of daily life? It occurred to me that sometimes being a good representative of the Kingdom hinges on the simplest things, almost trivial.

Let me give you an example from my own life.

I have had some of the most interesting conversations about spiritual matters with ordinary people who serve my table in restaurants. Since any contact with others is an opportunity to be an ambassador, I try to keep an eye open for what might turn out to be a "divine appointment."

This is something you can do, too. Here are some ways to set the stage to engage them in a friendly way.

First, find out the server's name.

This is easy if they're wearing a name tag. If not, simply ask. If it's a unique name or suggests some ethnic history, ask about it. It's a friendly thing to do—even flattering—and will help you remember the name better.

Begin to use their name immediately. If you're like me, it's difficult to keep track of names, especially of people you encounter for the short duration of a quick meal. But there are a few things that help.

For one, just the conscious effort itself may be enough to help you remember. Another way is to associate something new with something old. When you tie the new thing to something you already know, the job is much easier. In my case, if the waiter's name is Mike, I immediately think of my good friend and former tennis partner. That alone will temporarily fix the waiter's name in my mind.

The second thing I do is leave a decent tip.

My own standard is between 15% on the low end to 20% for really good service. Sure, sometimes a server doesn't deserve 15%. But if they get shorted by me on the tip, I think they're less likely to attribute it to their poor service than they are to associate bad tipping with stingy Christian patrons (the after-church crowd is notorious for stiffing the restaurant help).

There's one last thing I do, and it may be the most important. As I'm walking out, I make a point to find the waiter or waitress and simply say, "Thank you." It's a small gesture, but I want their last impression of me to be as pleasant as their first.

What's the real goal behind this modest effort? Simply this: People are important to the Lord, and if they are important to Him, they should be important to you and me.

Addressing people by their names and showing genuine appreciation for service are simple ways to show they are valued. This speaks volumes about the One you represent. Never underestimate the role of good manners.

How would they know I'm a Christian? Maybe they wouldn't. I don't always have a Bible with me, and I don't wear religious jewelry or shirts with Christian slogans.

However, since we always bow our heads to give thanks at our table, or the server may overhear snatches of conversation about spiritual things, it's certainly possible he'll make the connection. The last thing I want anyone to do is associate my prayer or my Bible or my Christian tract with rudeness, stinginess, or a demanding, high-maintenance customer.

It may be that the server and I never get around to spiritual matters. In point of fact, we usually don't. Even so, I still want to leave behind a "fragrant aroma" for the sake of Christ. That's one of the reasons Paul says in Colossians 3:17, "And whatever you do in word or deed, do all in the name of the Lord Jesus"—that is, as His representative and consistent with His wishes.

In His care,

Greg

Through Doors of Opportunity

Cheryl McGuinness is a unique Christian woman who has taught me something about going through doors of opportunity for Christ.

Cheryl's husband, Tom, was the co-pilot of American Airlines Flight 11, the first plane to hit the World Trade Center on September 11, 2001. He also was a student of Stand to Reason.[4] Cheryl and I had a touching conversation on our radio show soon after that tragedy.

Two things stood out for me about Cheryl McGuinness.

First, she is an "ordinary" follower of Christ, like most of us—living without any hunger for publicity, never having a desire for fame, never having ambitions to be in the limelight, especially for this reason.

Second, she has courageously chosen to do a very difficult thing—walk through the door of opportunity God had opened for her, even in the midst of her grief.

When the fate of the Jewish people hung in the balance and Queen Esther had a unique opportunity to act, her uncle Mordecai said to her, "And who knows whether you have not attained royalty for such a time as this?" (Esther 4:14b)

Mordecai understood that some things are not accidents, that God sovereignly orchestrates our affairs in ways we do not see nor immediately understand.

Cheryl McGuinness recognized that God had sovereignly put her in a unique position to make a difference for the Kingdom. It came through a tragedy that was thrust upon her. It came through pain and hardship. It came through grief and confusion. But when the door opened she said "yes" to Him and moved forward.

Of course, most of us won't be pushed into the spotlight as Cheryl had been. Yet I'm convinced that God opens small doors of opportunity— "divine appointments," some people call them— for each one of us on a regular basis.

There are only two things we need to do. First, begin to look to see if a door is swinging open a bit. Second, have the courage to step forward and step through it.

Most of us will probably not have media coverage, television appearances, or book deals. Instead, we'll take much smaller steps if we're alert for the opportunities and we're willing to let God push us out of our comfort zone a little.

Remember, the course of history is often changed by small things done by ordinary people at opportune times.

Ask a question to get things rolling, then see where it leads. Don't put yourself under a lot of pressure to go the distance. Just make the effort. Take the chance. Then see what God will do with your step of trust.

Be alert for what Lee Strobel calls "ricochet evangelism." You may be talking to one person, but the inconspicuous eavesdropper—a co-worker in the next cubicle, a family member on the periphery of the conversation—may be God's intended target.

Don't be too focused on results. Leave them to God. Just be faithful to respond to the opportunity. Outward appearances can be deceiving. A person may rebel at what you share, but if you're thoughtful in what you say and gracious in how you say it, chances are good you will have given him something to think about.

Sometimes you won't be in the mood. Sometimes you'll be inconvenienced. Sometimes your own emotional needs will begin to blind you to the opportunities.

At times like that, remember Cheryl. She had every reason to deal with her grief in solitude. Yet, when God opened a door of opportunity for her—even in painful circumstances—she stepped through it in trust.

Don't forget to take some small chances for the Kingdom. Do something for the Lord that may be a little frightening. Be willing to be stretched by putting yourself in an uncomfortable situation for the right reasons.

Walk through that door of opportunity.

Under His mercy,

Greg

Everybody's Problem

After decades of addressing the problem of evil, I have discovered an approach that has massively simplified my task, one that subtly turns the tables on atheists, hanging them—appropriately—on the horns of their own dilemma.

Here's how it works. I do not begin my response with *tactical* concerns (maneuvering on the specifics), but rather with a *strategic* point (sketching out the big picture) meant to show that the atheist himself is just as vulnerable to the problem of evil as he thinks the theist is. Maybe more so.

To set the stage, I begin by clarifying the challenge in vivid terms. I spell out the logic of the complaint. Then I offer an anecdote, an illustration, or a graphic piece of news (there's always some horror in the headlines) accentuating the gravity of the atheist's protest. In short, I try to *increase* the emotional force of the objection.

Next, I tell the audience I do not grapple with the problem first as a theologian, or as a philosopher, or even as a Christian, but as a human being trying to make sense of my world. Evidence of egregious evil abounds. How do I account for such depravity?

But, I am quick to add—and here is the strategic move—*I am not alone*. As a theist, I am not the only one saddled with this challenge. Evil is a problem *for everyone*. Since evil is an objective feature of the world (hence the objection), every person, regardless of religion or world view, must face its challenge. *Even the atheist.*

What if someone is assaulted by personal tragedy, distressed by world events, or victimized by religious corruption or abuse, and then responds by rejecting God and becoming an atheist (as many have done)? Notice that he has not *solved* the problem of evil. He has simply eliminated one possible answer to it: theism.

The atheist can't raise the issue, turn on his heel, and smugly walk away. His objection is that evil *actually* exists, objectively. Otherwise, why raise the complaint? Even if theism fails to give a satisfying answer, the problem doesn't disappear. Evil remains.

The atheist still has to answer the question, "How do I explain evil now, *as an atheist*? How do I answer the problem of evil *from a materialistic world view*?" He no longer has the resources of theism to draw from. So what is he left with?

There is only one solution for him. The atheist must play the relativism card. Morality is either the product of a social contract or a trick of evolution. That is the best materialism can do. His *own* answer to the problem of evil, then, is that there is no objective problem of evil. Morality is an illusion. Whatever is, is right. Nothing more can be said.

Do you see the difficult place this puts the atheist in? If this is the right answer to the problem of evil, then his initial complaint vanishes.

Why grouse about God just because some cultural group doesn't happen to approve of the current course of events? Why beef because our genes have conditioned us to feel bad when rapists rape and killers kill? The only evil that can get traction as a problem against God must be the real deal—objective evil—not something that is merely a cultural or biological invention.

Here's the irony. The existence of evil initially made the atheist furious, yet his own world view turns the objective evil he was so livid about into a complete illusion. This is a solution?

The great 20th century atheistic philosopher Bertrand Russell wondered how anyone could talk of God when kneeling at the bed of a dying child. His challenge has powerful rhetorical force. How can anyone cling to the hope of a benevolent, powerful sovereign in the face of such tragedy?

Then Christian philosopher William Lane Craig offered this response: "What is the atheist Bertrand Russell going to say when kneeling at the bed of a dying child? 'Too bad'? 'Tough luck'? 'That's the way it goes'?" No happy ending? No silver lining? Nothing but devastating, senseless evil?

Atheists are struck dumb in circumstances like this.

They cannot speak of the patience and mercy of God. They cannot mention the future perfection that awaits all who trust in Christ. They cannot offer the comfort that a redemptive God is working to cause all things to work together for good to those who love Him and are called according to His purpose. They have no "good news" of hope for a broken world. Their worldview denies them these luxuries.

Which brings me to the most important question to ask of the problem of evil: *Which world view has the best resources to make sense of this challenge?*

The answer is not atheism. The answer to evil is God—in Jesus, on a cross, at Calvary. The particulars still need to be worked out, and the apparent contradiction between evil and God still needs to be addressed. But I start with the strategic issue first. That sets the stage. Only afterward do I get into details.

With confidence in Christ,

Greg

Atheists' "Non-Belief"

Atheists no longer believe there is no God, apparently. Instead, they merely lack belief in the divine. They are not *un*-believers. They are simply *non*-believers. And non-belief is a passive state, not an active claim, so it requires no defense.

This—atheists think—makes their job easier by relieving them of any responsibility to provide evidence for their view, er…their non-view. After all, no one is obliged to give evidence for the non-existence of fairies. Thus, atheism secures the inside lane as the default view for reasonable people.

Or so atheists suppose.

If I were an atheist, I would never take this route. I'd fear people would think me cheating with words, betraying weakness, not strength. This, as it turns out, is exactly what's happening. Yes, there is a difference between non-belief and unbelief, but there is no refuge here for the atheist.

For example, if you asked me which rugby team was the best in England, I wouldn't know where to start. Since I have no interest in the question and no information on the issue, I have not formed a belief one way or another. Because I have no beliefs about the quality of rugby competition in the U.K., I am truly a non-believer regarding the question. I am neutral.

This is not the case with atheists. It's true, atheists have no belief *in* God, but they are not neutral on this question. If they were, they wouldn't be writing books or accepting invitations for debates. No one debates about non-beliefs. There would be nothing to talk about.

For an atheist to enter a debate, he has to take a position. If he takes a position, he asserts a belief. And when he asserts a belief, he makes a claim. When he advances an argument, presumably he believes the conclusion that flows from his own reasoning. Theists say there is a God, and atheists argue they are wrong. This is not neutrality.

To say you do not believe *in* God is very different from saying you lack belief *about* God. Anyone who has a point of view has a belief. And atheists have a point of view. This makes them believers of a very particular stripe: They believe God does not exist. They are not neutral.

There's another problem, though, that apparently has escaped the notice of those atheists who claim the high road of reason as their own. Given any proposition (e.g., "God exists"), there are only three possible responses to it. You can affirm it ("God does exist"), you can deny it ("God does not exist"), or you can withhold judgment ("I don't know"), either for lack of information or lack of interest or exposure (like my non-belief about English footballers).

In the God debate, those who affirm the proposition have always been called theists (of some sort). Those who deny it have been called atheists. Those who withhold have been called agnostics.

The alleged "non-beliefers" in question here are clearly neither in the first group nor the last. Only one logical option remains: They deny God exists, which is why they are called atheists. An atheist (from the Greek, *a-* for "not," and *theos*, for "God") is a person who holds "not God." That is an active claim, not a passive non-belief.

The only way out of this logical tri-lemma is to simply stand on the sidelines and not participate, either for lack of interest or for lack of information. However, neither apathy nor uncertainty seem to characterize those who say they "lack a belief in God."

Now, whether or not atheists are obliged to offer evidence for their denial is a different question. This brings us back to fairies. Atheists are not neutral on the question of fairies, either. They deny their existence, as do I. In my view, though, neither of us is obliged to give evidence *against* fairies because no plausible reason has ever been advanced *for* them, as far as I know.

That is not the case with God, however. Since 99% of the people in the world believe in God, then rejection of that which seems self-evident to virtually everyone on the planet requires some rationale, arguably, especially in light of the cogent arguments in favor of God's existence.

The atheist's unwillingness to step up to the plate on this smacks of intellectual timidity and dishonesty. Since they claim to be champions of reason (the "brights," to use Daniel Dennett's euphemism for his kind), then they ought to live according to its rules, it seems to me.

For the Kingdom,

Greg

Morality and Monopoly

Recently I've run into a challenge to my own challenge of moral relativism.[5] The rejoinder is clever, but misleading. I want to give you my response so you will be ready for it if you encounter the same objection.

First a quick review.

Moral relativism is the view that ideas of right and wrong are more like ice cream than insulin. Saying certain conduct is wrong is like saying vanilla tastes bad. The statement only tells you what individual people like. It says nothing about the action itself. There can be as many moral "truths," then, as there are people (or cultures) who believe them.

Consequently, moral relativism is a kind of subjectivism. When it comes to moral rules—principles of right and wrong—it's up to the subject, the individual, to decide because there are no true, universal, ethical obligations or moral principles that apply equally to all people.

Note, by the way, that the "subject" can be an individual person or a group of people, even a whole culture. Most relativism today is the latter sort. Right and wrong are socially constructed by the group. However, since no universal standard exists to govern all groups, each decides right and wrong only for itself without judging those that hold other values.

Even with this brief description, I think you can see a problem beginning to emerge. A relativist is not going to be able to get any traction if he wants to condemn (in any ultimate sense) any behavior, regardless how evil it seems to be. In the final analysis, as with ice cream, one action is just as "good" as the other. There is no objective right or wrong, evil or good, virtue or vice. Anything goes.

Since this is the relativist's fatal weakness, I'm not surprised when I get pushback on this point. "No relativist believes that anything goes," I've been told. "You're twisting our view. Every culture has its own framework of right and wrong. Even if there are no universal standards of morality, that doesn't mean it's a free-for-all within a given group."

Fair enough. Let me answer this charge with a simple illustration.

Let us pretend that you want to play the classic board game, Monopoly. Like every other game, Monopoly has rules. There are standards, a framework of right or wrong of sorts that works within the Monopoly "community." According to the rules of the game, for example, you cannot have houses and hotels on the same piece of property. That would be wrong. The inventors of the game said so.

Relativism is like Monopoly. In one sense, it's not the case that "anything goes." Rather, standards set by the community (Parker Brothers, in this case) govern behavior.

These laws are "true," though, in an entirely different way than, say, the laws of gravity are true. They are not true because of the way the world is structured, but because of the way human beings (subjects) have arranged the game. If you don't like the rules, you can change them (variations that are sometimes called "house rules"), or play a different game, or play no game at all. It's completely up to you.

You can't do that with gravity. If you don't like the laws of physics, too bad. Adapt or die. Reality will punish you if you don't take it seriously.

Yes, even in relativistic systems you can get punished by the group if you break the rules and get caught. But I think you can see this is a contrived sort of "punishment" based merely on human conventions ("Go directly to Jail. Do not pass Go. Do not collect $200."), not on transcendent standards.

In the end, as I said, anything goes. That's always the case with relativism.

If you are a moral realist (an objectivist), you think moral rules are real things, not individual whims or social conventions created by culture. They are like gravity, not like Monopoly. If you are a relativist, you are playing Monopoly with right and wrong.

Of course, this would not make relativism false. It might be that, given the nature of the world, all we are left with when it comes to ethics are human conventions. But if that's the case, then an intellectually honest relativist will have to admit that.

Given the relativist's view of the world, then, ultimately anything goes.

Yours because His,

Greg

The Power of Simple Proverbs

A few years back a close friend of mine launched a cottage industry making calendars and desk accessories.

His products are called Demotivators. They take a tongue-in-cheek shot at the slick motivational posters with breathtaking photos, single-word titles like "Teamwork" or "Excellence," and short captions meant to launch productivity.

Despair, Inc.'s approach is different. For example, a vivid stop-action photo of a boxer taking a knock-out punch on the chin opines on "Agony" and warns, "Not all pain is gain."

Short adages like this one pack a lot of punch in a few words. They capitalize on the power of pithy statements to change thinking and generate action. Nike's three short words "Just do it" have frequently snapped me out of my own indolence and sloth.

A good ambassador stays alert for words of wisdom like these: a proverb or an adage that motivates to action or to careful, thoughtful, virtuous living. They keep them handy—or commit them to memory—for times when a prod or an encouragement is necessary.

Last week I was dragging my feet on a distasteful project (like most people, I have my bouts with laziness and lethargy). I kept putting it off until I read this line from Ben Franklin's *Poor Richard's Almanac*: "All things are easy to industry, all things difficult to sloth." Suddenly I realized that my procrastination took more energy than the task itself. By contrast, decisive action takes much of the pain out of the work. I quickly completed the job.

This is the power of proverbs. I don't mean just the Bible's Proverbs, though they certainly qualify. I mean any short, pithy aphorism that, in a clever and memorable way, captures an insight about wise living. Something about the snappy wording of these witticisms motivates action.

That's one of the reasons I was so excited about a book I read and reread with relish, a book filled with real-world ambassador wisdom: *In, But Not Of*, by Hugh Hewitt. It's a series of short vignettes meant to stoke the fires of productive ambition.

In Hewitt's own words, "This is a book about earthly power in the service of those engaged in the big battle." He has written it for aspiring Christian ambassadors, especially those whose arena of impact is more outside the church than in—which is most of us. It captures STR's "knowledge, wisdom, and character" principles succinctly and passionately.

The book's descriptive chapter titles sometimes tell the whole story on a key aspect of being an ambassador: "Disclose the Weak Points in Your Argument and Deal with Them," "Be Slow to Be Offended," "Coasting Will Kill You," "Know What You Don't Know."

Feast on these insights:

- **On discipline:** Most of the free world is managed by disciplined people who rise early and work late, and who take pleasure in their craft.

- **On being winsome:** Ask at least a half-dozen questions in every conversation. Interested is interesting.

- **On humility:** The hardest words for some people to learn to say or write are "I don't know." So practice them. The fellow who is quick to admit what he doesn't know is much more likely to be believed when he asserts his expertise.

- **On tactics:** The best advocates anticipate and meet the strongest objections to their arguments rather than hope opponents will not raise them or superiors will not see them.

- **On community:** Choose a church and join it—genuinely. There is no perfect fit. But you must find a fit, no matter where you live or how often you move.

- **On productivity:** Life is a habit. Remember that. Life is a habit.

I wish I had read Hugh's book—or something like it—35 years ago. You don't have to wait that long. If you want to learn how to plan your life for impact, start with a handful of simple proverbs. Then add more.

Remember, life is a habit. And habits like this one build effective ambassadors.

For the Kingdom,

Greg

Banning "Faith"

I have frequently encouraged Christians to ban words like "faith" and "belief" from their vocabulary. They're too easily misunderstood. Instead, use the language of truth during your moments of truth so there's no confusion.

Simply put: Talk about facts, not faith. In today's culture, people take "faith" and "belief" as religious wishful thinking, not the kind of intelligent step of trust the Bible has in mind when it uses those terms.

I had a chance to put my own advice into practice in front of a national TV audience. The occasion was a full hour of crossfire-style debate hosted by Christian apologist Lee Strobel. My opponent was New Age guru Deepak Chopra, the best-selling author of more than 20 million books.[6]

Strobel's opening question to me was, "Greg, what do you think the future of faith looks like?"

This is exactly the kind of situation I'm concerned about—the word "faith" twisting in the wind in all its troublesome ambiguity. Here was the essence of my response:

Lee, we have to be clear on what we mean by "the future of faith." We could mean "the future of religion"—faith as a noun—or we could mean "the future of acts of trust"—faith as a verb.

In one sense, the future of religion is the same as it's ever been. If your religious beliefs are accurate, there is tremendous hope. But if your religious views are false, if you're taking a leap of faith trusting in fantasy, there is no hope.

Whatever was true 1000 years ago about religion is true today. Reality doesn't change just because beliefs change. And reality has a way of bruising those who don't take it seriously. This is why Christianity has never encouraged a leap of faith.

If we get reality wrong and trust in a fantasy, we're going to get injured. Our job is to do the best we can to get the facts right, to have accurate religious views—faith as a noun—then act consistently with those facts—faith as a verb.

So, if truth is your goal, I'm optimistic about the future of faith. If not—if people turn instead to leaps of faith and wishful thinking—then I'm pessimistic.

This was my opening salvo. A vigorous debate followed. From the outset, though, I wanted to set the tone. Regardless of whatever Dr. Chopra had in mind, as a Christian I was interested in reality, in truth—not in rosy fantasies or wishful thinking.

By contrast, Chopra championed feelings and experience over religious doctrine and dogma. This is dangerous advice.

Mark this: *Feelings make life beautiful, but careful thinking—reason—makes life safe.*

Feelings are misleading indicators of truth. People can feel safe even when in desperate peril. They can also feel completely conflicted and distraught when doing what is right.

This is like the used car salesman who tells you, "Drive the car, but don't look under the hood." You may enjoy the ride for the moment, but you'll never know if he's selling you a lemon or not.

Never trust anyone who tells you to rely on experience over right thinking. Most requests to banish judgments come just before someone says or does something that ought to be judged.

They say, "Experience, not reason is the best guide for truth," just before making claims you should be inspecting very carefully when they're telling you not to. They discourage you from using the tools necessary to separate good from evil, safety from silliness, wisdom from peril.

In life there are lots of lemons. And many of them are spiritually deadly. "Look before you leap" is sage advice. It applies especially to leaps of faith.

In His kindness,

Greg

When Good Is Evil

I would like you to consider for a moment how something can be good and evil at the same time. Then I want to explain why this insight is so vital for you as an ambassador of Christ.

At first glance, to say something is simultaneously good and not good (evil) sounds like a contradiction. There is no conflict, though, if the thing is good in one way, and not good in an entirely different way. It is possible, for example, for something to render benefit in the short term, but have devastating consequences as time wears on.

A man with cancer can take morphine to reduce his physical suffering. In a temporal sense, that's good. He feels better. His distress has departed. He is sedate and calm instead of crippled by pain.

But what if the artificial sense of well-being induced by the drug dissuades him from receiving the therapy necessary to heal him? The morphine cannot correct the disease; it only covers it. If no further steps are taken, the malignancy eventually kills him.

Can we say that the morphine is really good if

it eliminates the symptom, but the patient dies from the disease? No. Ultimately, it is destructive. If relief from pain keeps a man from remedial surgery, then the relief can't be called good. Whenever a soothing remedy substitutes for health-giving therapy, evil results.

This is true of everything. A fine meal laced with arsenic is delicious, but deadly. The good thing is also evil. A casual sexual encounter may be satisfying in the moment, but with STDs or unwanted pregnancies the apparent "goodness" is eclipsed by the ultimate result.

Here's why this insight is important. As you grow as an ambassador for Christ you will face the growing challenge of religious pluralism— the idea that religion is a good thing since each ultimately lead to God. Generally, those who promote the inherent goodness of religion do not appreciate the good/evil tradeoff I've just described.

Alternate religions might offer effective guidelines to moral living. That's good as far as it goes. It's good to live righteously. Right living contributes to physical and emotional health. Those who continually practice sin eventually suffer its consequences.

The problem is, it doesn't go far enough. If a given religion is wrong about the eternal consequences, then it cannot be called "good" in spite of the short term benefit it offers. The final analysis is what really counts. Any temporally "good" thing, including religion, must be measured not by its immediate effect, but by its ultimate result.

The fact is, our most valiant attempts at goodness are met with failure because a deep-seated malignancy sucks the life from our efforts. No matter how hard we try, each of us is dying from a spiritual disease that no amount of righteous living can repel.

Therefore, every religious system that promotes righteous behavior *as an ultimate end*—Judaism, Islam, Mormonism, and even Christianity in certain forms—is treating the symptom and not the disease.

If the Christian view is accurate, then every human being, from the greatest to the least, has broken God's law. That makes us all guilty, and guilty people must seek God's surgery: the new birth that follows forgiveness. Agreed, some need more forgiveness than others—sometimes much more, just as disease can ravage one body more violently than another—but every person is fatally stricken, nonetheless.

Any religion that grants a temporal benefit while robbing of an eternal deliverance is poison, no matter how good or decent it looks in the short term. Thus, we are never free to call religion good in the final sense. That which seemed good in the moment has become evil.

To rephrase Marx (Karl, not Groucho), *false* religion is the opiate of the people. It soothes, but does not cure.

Under His mercy,

Greg

Religious Placebos

I once opened my talk before a group in Southern California with a "profound" observation: There's a difference between ice cream and insulin.[7]

When choosing ice cream, you choose what you like. When choosing medicine, you choose what heals. When choosing ice cream you choose what's true for you. When choosing medicine you choose what's true.

Here's how that observation cashes out for you and me. Americans think of God, religion, and morals like ice cream and not like insulin. They choose religious views according to tastes, according to what they prefer, rather than according to what's true.

"The freedom of our day," lamented a graduate in a Harvard commencement address, "is the freedom to devote ourselves to any values we please, on the mere condition that we do not believe them to be true."[8]

Yes, non-believers view religion like ice cream. Remarkably, Christians frequently do the same. Our offer of Jesus is often not based on truth grounded in evidence—as it was with the early disciples of Christ—but on mere experience.

Jesus used to be hard medicine for a deadly disease: sin. Now in many circles He's been reduced to a tasty dish, a pleasant meal, a more delicious alternative: "Try Him; you'll like Him."

Sharing our experience has some advantages. First, it's easy. Second, convictions based on experience are hard to defeat. As one wag put it, "The man with an argument is always at the mercy of a man with an experience." Beliefs based on experience are extremely difficult to uproot. This is not always a virtue, though. Sometimes it's a vice. Here's why.

Our He-works-for-me approach may give us false security. It protects us from attack—no one can take our experience away from us—but experience alone is compromised as a test for truth since subjective elements often equally affirm contradictory notions, both truth and error.

How can we be confident our experiences are reliable guides? And if Jesus is our "flavor," what relevance does that have for someone who actually takes the question of truth seriously, like many atheists?

In *Skeptic* magazine, atheist Lawrence Hyman wrote that the defenders of the truth of God and religion...

> ...no longer insist on His existence as an objective truth, but on His presence to *them*....Many religious people defend their truths by reference to the power of [experience] to console *them* and to give meaning to *their* lives. How can anyone argue against the existence of a subjective experience?[9] [emphasis in the original]

Hyman ends by saying atheism is no longer

relevant. That sounds like good news, but it's not. It's bad news when you consider his reason.

The reason atheism is no longer relevant is because truth is no longer relevant, even to religious people. This "death of truth" portends not just the death of atheism, but the death of Christianity, as well.

If moral and religious truth are subjective—merely *true for us*—there can be no conflict between moralities or religions. All are equally true to the people who hold them.

If this is our message, then Christians are no different from anyone else with a religious placebo—some belief that simply makes them feel better.

This kind of Christianity may be able to soothe, but it can never heal. Hyman the atheist understands what many Christians have yet to realize: Truth matters.

Even atheists know there is a difference between insulin and ice cream.

Your partner for truth,

Greg

"Hearing" from God

A group of 40 leaders of a local church gathered together on a Friday evening to discuss the spiritual malaise of their congregation and how to correct it. For three hours they pooled their wisdom, with dozens of ideas being tossed into the ring.

So many provocative options were suggested there was no time left for assessment, so they agreed to meet again to evaluate the proposals that had surfaced that evening.

Just as the pastor began to close in prayer, someone stopped him with an observation. "We've been talking now for three hours," he said, "but we've never once asked God what His opinion was."

Murmurs of approval spread through the group. "We can all hear from God," a woman added. "Let's be sure this is really His decision for our church and not just human wisdom."

Another suggested they all fast the day before the next meeting to ensure God would speak to them. Some confided they didn't feel comfortable making judgments of this magnitude. This one was God's call.

Consider the spiritual convictions expressed at that meeting in light of the strong words Paul had for Christians living in Corinth who seemed incapable of resolving the disputes that divided them. Here is what Paul wrote in 1 Corinthians 6:1-6:

> Does any one of you, when he has a case against his neighbor, dare to go to law before the unrighteous, and not before the saints? Or *do you not know* that the saints will judge the world? And if the world is judged by you, are you not *competent* to constitute the smallest law courts? *Do you not know* that we shall judge angels? How much more, matters of this life? If then you have law courts dealing with matters of this life, do you appoint them as judges who are of no account in the church? *I say this to your shame*. Is it so, that there is not among you *one wise man who will be able to decide*…?

Paul was deeply disturbed that these Christians had turned to gentiles to solve their problems. Note, though, the apostle's antidote. He did not direct them to "hear from God," the solution that seemed so apt to the Friday gathering of leaders.

On the contrary, to Paul it was a matter of shame that because of ignorance of certain important truths (twice he said "Or do you not know….") these Christians did not have the competence to handle this on their own, that there was not a single person among them with wisdom adequate to the task.

The mistake made that Friday evening is a common one, partly because it seems so right: Let God decide for us. That's the safest course of action. Our best efforts should be spent learning to hear from God instead of pooling our "fleshly" human wisdom.

Though popular, this spiritual principle—getting a personal word from God to decide our course of action—is never taught in the Bible. Instead, the standard Paul laid down in 1 Corinthians 6—knowledge coupled with wisdom—is taught in many places and was consistently modeled by the apostles themselves.

It did not seem to occur to the group that night that if it were up to God to decide for them, then *all that evening's discussion had been wasted*. When God speaks, all human mouths are silenced. There is nothing more to add.

Further, *God had already spoken* giving all the knowledge needed to direct their choices, but they had ignored it. Never once was a passage of Scripture invoked as a source of guidance on the question before them. Ironically, this oversight was possibly the very thing responsible for the spiritual lassitude their church had been pondering in the first place.

How often do Christians labor to hear God speaking, yet apply little effort to understanding what He has already said? What makes us think we're entitled to a private word from God when the Word He has already given has been ignored?

You and I cannot be equipped to defend the truth unless we know the truth beyond mere generalities. If we learn to employ God's Word accurately to inform our decisions as ambassadors for Christ, then when God asks again, "Is there not one wise man among you," He will not be answered with silence.

In His grip,

Greg

Do Not Fear Them

Lately I have had to fight my impulse to whine, to pout, to play the victim. I am not happy with recent developments.

It was bad enough when the Massachusetts Supreme Court nullified, by judicial fiat, thousands of years of natural order when they demanded the state legislature draft laws that would solemnize marriage between homosexual couples. Then virtually overnight a geyser of marriage licenses for same-sex couples erupted from city hall in San Francisco. Soon other cities followed suit.

We finally elect a president with the moral clarity to sign a ban on the barbaric procedure known as partial-birth abortion, then a judge slaps an injunction on it before the ink has dried. Meanwhile, more babies die.

Chuck Colson warned that just when postmodernism is losing credibility in secular society, the church openly embraces this radical form of relativism.[10]

Then Brian McLaren, Christian writer, pastor, and promoter of the postmodern "emergent church" movement, delivers a sizzling broadside on Colson. In an open letter, he belittles Colson's understanding of postmodernism and hails his own version as a welcome correction to the arrogance of Evangelicalism.

Every time I turn around, it seems, another book, article, or seminar teaches believers how to "hear" the voice of God speaking to them personally. Yet those same Christians stay mired in biblical illiteracy, not knowing the Word of God that has already been spoken because their "seeker sensitive" churches have not taken seriously Jesus' command to build disciples.

Am I the only one who's fighting discouragement? What is happening here?

There's a simple answer to that question and a simple explanation for why we often feel outmatched and out-maneuvered at every turn, a simple reason why the scoreboard always seems to read: Lions 10, Christians 0. Listen to Jesus:

> A disciple is not above his teacher, nor a slave above his master. If they have called the head of the house Beelzebub, how much more the members of his household (Matthew 10:24 ff).

Jesus warned us in advance. This is exactly how our Savior was treated, and this is exactly what He said our lot would be.

We should never expect a fair shake, nor whine when it is not given. We are not to play the victim. That is disloyalty to Christ. "Followers of Christ flinch at times from the pain of wounds and the smart of slights," Os Guinness wrote, "but that cost is in the contract of the way of the cross....No child of a sovereign God whom we can call our Father is ever a victim or in a minority."[11]

This is why Jesus finished His comments with, "Therefore, do not fear them, for there is nothing covered that will not be revealed, and hidden that will not be known."

Listen carefully to those last words: *"Do not fear them."* Jesus is with us. And He promises a final day of reckoning. As one person put it, "There is a justice, and one day they shall feel it." But even ultimate victory should not be our chief concern.

If you want to know how to fight off discouragement, consider these words of Alan Keyes: "It is not for us to calculate our victory or fear our defeat, but to do our duty and leave the rest in God's hands."

As Christians we measure our legitimacy by faithfulness and obedience to Christ, who alone will bring the increase. The most important gauge of our success will not be our numbers or even our impact, but our fidelity to Jesus.

When the odds are against us, we do not quit or even slow down. We fight. We do not fear the opposition. We do not whine, or pout, or play the victim. We take what comes our way, hold our heads high, and stay engaged. Because of Jesus' promise, we are of good cheer:

> These things I have spoken to you, that in Me you may have peace. In the world you have tribulation, but take courage; I have overcome the world. John 16:33

Warmly in Christ,

Greg

Two Conversations at Normandy

While teaching in France one year, I made a trip by train to the Normandy coast to visit the D-Day battlegrounds. While there, I had two separate encounters with strangers that each illustrate a valuable lesson about being an ambassador for Christ.

Roger was a Brit on vacation with his wife and his teenage son and daughter. I met him at a small sidewalk café in Bayeux, a little French village that served as a jumping off point for tours to Utah Beach.

When Roger learned I was lecturing in Strasbourg on religion he piped up, "In order to be religious you have to have faith." He gestured disdainfully at his wife. "She has it; we don't." I glanced over at her, the sole believer in the family. She smiled back timidly.

Roger correctly understood the need for faith, but he was confused on what faith was. To him, faith was a mysterious ability certain people possessed to believe ridiculous things and feel good about it. Some people had it (his wife); some didn't (he and his children).

Roger needed to know that faith isn't an ability that some people have and others lack. Instead, faith is a reasoned response of trust, the kind of step we all take in thousands of ordinary ways every day. The more evidence we have—the more good reasons we have—the easier our step of trust is going to be.

Christian faith is not a force and it's not some kind of magic. It is simple trust in the One who has the power. People sometimes say, "My faith carried me through." But that's not true at all. Faith can't carry anything. It can only grab on to God's extended hand. He does the rest. God carries us through.

The lesson: Be equipped to clearly explain the nature of biblical faith.

My second encounter taught me a completely different lesson. Steve and I were the lone travelers on a bus from Bayeux to the American cemetery at Colleville. He was from Arizona traveling on his own. Our chat quickly turned to weighty matters. Though a non-Christian, he was very open to what I had to say about Christ.

Steve's background was in philosophy. He'd thought carefully about what he considered to be the respectable claims of Christianity. And he was very aware of the inadequacies of pop religious philosophies, including relativism and religious pluralism. He also had little respect for Christians who tried to have it both ways—embracing Jesus as *their* truth, but acknowledging other religions as just as legitimate.

Steve the non-believer had a better grasp of classical Christianity than many believers. He knew that if Christianity were true, then Jesus was insulin, not ice cream. He understood that when believers retreat from the clear claims of the Gospel, they may sound more politically correct, but they no longer have a healing message. Ice cream can't cure anything.

The lesson: Don't relativize the Gospel. When confronted with such a watered-down message, the more astute non-Christian will recognize the inherent cowardice in the move and lose respect for the messenger.

Your partner for truth,

Greg

Choosing Your Battles

I once had a Christian friend whose boss, a lesbian, posed a difficult question to her. She wanted to know what my friend's attitude was toward homosexuality.

Now that's a tough one because as a Christian she has strong views on the issue. At the same time, she was concerned that expressing her own personal views to her employer (for whom the question was not merely academic) might compromise her situation.

My friend's response was, "Please tell me what my feelings about homosexuality have to do with our professional relationship?"

In sword fighting that's called a parry. She deflected her boss's question, pushing it aside by asking about its relevance. Because she was quick, my friend avoided what might have been an unpleasant confrontation.

It was a fair response. Sometimes you're asked a personal question when it's not the best time to express your opinion. When we make our case about the Lord or our religious or ethical views, we want to choose the time and place so we can be the most sensitive to the person we're talking to. We don't want our views misunderstood or twisted.

In less-than-ideal circumstances it's entirely fair to say, "You know, I'm not really comfortable offering my point of view at this time," or something like that. Or, as my friend did, "Could you clarify what this has to do with our relationship?"

My friend had successfully parried the issue for the moment, but suspected it would come up again. She might not be able to sidestep it twice. What should she do?

Here's what I suggested. Her answer would depend on precisely how the question was put to her. "How do you *feel* about homosexuality?" is different from, "What do you *think* about homosexuality?"

If someone asked me what I *felt* about homosexuality, I'd answer honestly: Though the behavior is discomfiting to me (I'm heterosexual, after all), I don't *feel* uncomfortable simply because someone is homosexual. Some homosexuals are likable, some are not. I deal with people as individuals.

If I were asked what I *think* about homosexuality, however, my answer would be different. I *think* that homosexuals are human beings who should be treated with respect, should not be bashed or called names, and should be given the same individual rights any other citizen has. That's what I actually think.

I also think that homosexuality is unnatural, unhealthy—physically and psychologically—and immoral. I say this not as a personal preference, but as a personal conviction—I think that statement is accurate and true. I'm also glad to give the reasons why I think so. These are my *thoughts* about homosexuality, as opposed to my *feelings*.

What this approach does is make a distinction between my attitude about homosexual *people* and my point of view regarding *homosexuality*.

When dealing with issues in the public square, it's important to make this distinction because people may mistakenly infer your feelings from your thoughts. If you start off by saying, "I think homosexuality is immoral," or "I think homosexuality is sin," people may infer from your ethical conclusions about homosexuality that you actually hate homosexuals, or that you are condescending towards them, etc. And, of course, they'd take offense.

Don't go down that road. You don't want to hide your moral point of view, but you also don't want them to draw wrong conclusions about your feelings—and how you might be inclined to treat homosexuals—from your moral assessment of homosexuality. By offering how you feel about homosexuality up front, you minimize that risk.

Choose your battles wisely. Don't allow yourself to be pushed into a conflict you're not prepared to handle.

Under His mercies,

Greg

The Magic Prayer

Over the years I've become increasingly disenchanted with the so-called "sinner's prayer." Found at the end of gospel tracts, it's also frequently used by pastors and evangelists as part of an altar call to usher the penitent into the Kingdom.

It goes something like this: "Lord Jesus, I am a sinner. I believe that You died for my sins so I could be forgiven. I receive You as my Lord and Savior. Thank You for coming into my life. Amen."

The prayer itself is fine. I prayed a version of it in 1973, initiating my own walk with Christ. I've used it since to assist others in expressing their faith for the first time. But it has a liability.

On occasion, I notice an almost superstitious disposition towards the prayer. It usually surfaces during a conversation about a wayward friend or member of the family. When I ask about their spiritual convictions, I am given this assurance: "Well, they prayed the prayer."

No, they're not living as Christians (ergo the problems), but they're still "in," presumably, saved by the power of the prayer. They recited the words and the words will do their work.

This seems to me a misplaced confidence.

I wonder if we've inoculated a whole generation of people who got a partial injection of Christianity and are now resistant to the real thing. They prayed the sinner's prayer, got their "fire insurance," and then faded back into the population. When confronted with the Gospel anew they shrug, "Been there, done that. Leave me alone. I have a life to live."

Let me suggest an antidote: The goal of evangelism should never be getting someone to *pray a prayer*. Rather, we should encourage them to *follow Jesus*. Our sense of safety can't come from simply repeating a series of words, even if well-intentioned at the time. When we emphasize *deciding* for Christ instead of *living* for Him, we often get spiritual miscarriages instead of spiritual births.

How, then, do we know if any person truly belongs to Christ? Our confidence comes from three sources.

The first is entirely subjective. Christians have an ineffable awareness that they belong to God. This comes from the witness of the Holy Spirit to our inner man: "For you have not received a spirit of slavery leading to fear again, but you have received a spirit of adoption as sons by which we cry out, 'Abba! Father!' The Spirit Himself bears witness with our spirit that we are children of God" (Romans 8:15-16).

John echoes the same thought when he writes, "By this we know that we abide in Him and He in us, because He has given us of His Spirit" (1 John 4:13).

Some people put the greatest emphasis on this subjective element, but the Scripture emphasizes it the least. The reason is, I think, because it's the most unreliable. Groups as theologically diverse as Evangelicals, Mormons, Jews, and New Agers lay claim to this confidence, but they can't all be correct.

Clearly, it's possible to have tremendous inner tranquility even when in extreme danger. Conversely, even the sturdiest spiritual warrior experiences periods of dryness, emptiness, and doubt.[12] Something more is necessary.

The second source of confidence in our salvation is the objective promise of Scripture based on the merits of Jesus. The apostle John's guarantee is characteristic, "These things I have written to you *who believe in the name of the Son of God*, in order that you may *know* that you have eternal life" (1 John 5:13).

This concept is so foundational it is repeated many times in the New Testament:

> John 3:16 For God so loved the world, that He gave His only begotten Son, that whoever believes in Him should not perish, but have eternal life.

> John 3:36 He who believes in the Son has eternal life, but he who does not obey the Son shall not see life, but the wrath of God abides on him.

> John 6:40 For this is the will of My Father, that everyone who beholds the Son and believes in Him, may have eternal life and I Myself will raise him up on the last day.

> Romans 10:9 If you confess with your mouth Jesus as Lord, and believe in your heart that God raised Him from the dead, you shall be saved.

The third—and most demonstrative—evidence of salvation is a holy life of persevering adherence to the Gospel of truth. John says bluntly, "The one who says, 'I have come to know Him,' and does not keep His commandments, is a liar" (1 John 2:4). Paul warns Timothy, "If we endure, we shall also reign with Him. If we deny Him, He also will deny us" (2 Timothy 2:12). Peter tells us to "be all the more diligent to make certain about His calling and choosing you, for as long as you practice these things, you will never stumble" (2 Peter 1:10).

The book of Hebrews is filled with warnings. "We have become partakers of Christ, if we hold fast the beginning of our assurance firm until the end" (3:14), and, "You have need of endurance, so that when you have done the will of God, you may receive what was promised" (10:36).

This is why the teaching of James is so important. Paul's instruction on justification by faith alone is so radical it can be mistaken for license, a charge he defends against in Romans 6:1-2. There's no such confusion with James, though. To paraphrase James 2:26, "The human body without the breath of life is nothing but a corpse. The same is true for anyone who says he has faith, but doesn't back it up with a changed life."

Our confidence that we belong to Christ is based on faith in God's promise evidenced by our perseverance. It is the engine that pulls the train. Our feelings are the caboose. The caboose is dispensable; the engine is not.

What makes a person sure his salvation is in force? If all he can say is "I prayed the prayer," or "I really feel God is in my life," he may be in trouble. People grow at different speeds, true enough, but there must be evidence of a life being transformed at some level.

If his confidence isn't based in the Gospel of truth, and if he's not actively following Jesus, we can give little assurance. The most loving thing we can do for a person like that is give him a sober warning.

If you want to lead someone to Christ, you may want to bypass the sinners prayer. There's no precedence for it in the Bible, anyway. In the New Testament, baptism served the function of marking a person's entry into the Body of Christ.

Rather, enjoin the one who is spiritually hungry to satisfy his appetite day by day by trusting and following the Savior. Give him some guidelines on how to do that. Tell him about prayer, fellowship, and Bible study. Instruct him in forgiveness, regeneration, and justification.

Don't let him forget, though, that being born again is the beginning, not the end.

Confident in the truth,

Greg

Ridiculed for Your Faith

I hadn't done anything like this in decades.

"Over there," he said, pointing to a bare patch of concrete adjacent to the heaviest flow of humanity. "Actually, you can pick any spot you want. Just let 'em have it. Pretty soon you'll have lots of people to argue with. Trust me."

It was Bruin Walk, the epicenter of foot traffic at noon at UCLA. It was my job to create a traffic jam by talking. About Jesus. Really loud.

The setting took me back to the spring of 1975. My brother Mark was cloaked in a tattered robe, thorns crowning his brow and "blood" dripping down his face. Over his shoulder was a rough-hewn cross he dragged up the steep incline of Bruin Walk. Behind him a Roman centurion goaded him on with a whip.

I was strategically positioned at the edge of the crowd with a few other Christians ready to "divide and conquer." As people began to jeer and sling insults at the religious street theater spectacle, we'd turn and engage the hecklers in conversation. Crazy.

But I was older now, more sophisticated. I lecture, I don't street preach.

I'd planned to speak on relativism during a campus group's evangelism week. But there was no podium, no lecture hall, no audience of beaming faces waiting to be impressed with my eloquence.

It slowly began to dawn on me that I was the heavy, the loud-mouth brought in to break up the hardened ground so the other believers could plant seeds. Except that most of the local faithful didn't show up. There were no other Christians mingling with the crowd to divide and conquer. I was all alone.

"So this was what Paul meant by 'living sacrifice'," I thought.

No question, I was shaken. For one fleeting moment I thought, "How am I going to get out of this?" But the Lord had boxed me in.

The trick was how to start. What was I going to say? I looked around, waiting for a cue, as if by some divine touch the sea of students milling around would suddenly part, the mob would grow quiet, and all eyes would respectfully fasten upon me.

I realized there was no easy entry. Like taking a dip in an icy pond, there's no way to slip in comfortably. I'd just have to jump. And jump I did.

The number one rule in a situation like this is to start with gusto. When you're scared spitless and feeling timid, raise your voice, bang the podium, beat your chest. In other words...fake it.

If I showed the least bit of fear or intimidation there'd be a feeding frenzy, and I'd be the main course. I had to *sound* confident even if I didn't *feel* confident.

Here's how I started. I pumped up my most impressive baritone and bellowed, "I don't know where all you Christians are, but I'm fed up with you. Usually there's a bunch of you hanging around these tables trying to shove your garbage down our throats, passing judgment, telling other people how to live. Why don't you leave us alone? Why are you always trying to drum up new business?"

The crowd quieted down and started listening. I began citing the offenses of the "bigoted Christian Right." I piled on criticisms layer by layer. As I did, I heard a couple of mock "amens" from the audience. They *liked* me attacking Christians.

I paused for effect, then continued.

"That was my voice 22 years ago when I was a student like you on this campus. I thought all Christians were dumb or ugly—or both. I had all the standard objections, the same ones I just listed."

Then for the next 45 minutes I talked. First I told them how Jesus changed my life. I spoke of the evil in my heart, the goodness and mercy of God, and my ultimate rescue. Then I fielded challenges.

I'd like to tell you about the revival that followed, but I can't because none did. I was just another Christian telling the truth, a truth no one seemed interested in that day. Not much had changed in 20 years. Except me.

Earlier, when I realized what I was up against that afternoon, I thought about the Apostle Paul.

He'd done this kind of thing all the time against much greater opposition. I asked myself, "What's the worst thing that can happen?" I wasn't going to get beheaded. I wouldn't be whipped, beaten, or stoned, as he had been.

No, a worse possibility awaited me. I could stumble around looking like an idiot. I could feel like a dope. People might roll their eyes. Some might even ignore me. Here I was inviting ridicule. For what?

For this: I had the truth; they didn't. I had the Lord; they were lost. I had nothing to be ashamed of; they had nothing. I was on a campus filled with desperate people believing foolish things. I had the truth that could rescue them, the truth of Jesus Christ crucified for their sins. And I was His ambassador. Looking foolish was a small price to pay to be faithful to that message.

Paul told the Philippians that if his life should be poured out as an offering for their faith, that was all right with him (Phil. 2:17). His pride was expendable for the Gospel's sake. His comfort was expendable. *He* was expendable.

Early on as a Christian I made a promise. I vowed I would never allow myself to be embarrassed to be associated with Jesus. I'm glad I crossed that bridge early, because I've had to make good on that promise many times since.

I have a suggestion for you. Why don't you make that promise, too, right now? Promise to never let yourself be ashamed to be a Christian. Remember, you have the truth. They don't. You have the Lord. They're lost. You have nothing to be ashamed of. They have nothing.

A lot of time has passed since those early days. But though I've grown older (and grayer), I'm just as passionate about the truth. And I am more convinced than ever about the importance of that truth clearly, graciously, and persuasively communicated. That's why I still jump in when God gives me the opportunity, even when I'm shaking in my boots.

If I could do that—then and now—so can you.

Step up to the front lines. You'll find it both challenging and exciting. If you take my invitation, God will reward you for jumping in for His kingdom with your witness for Him.

And if you "fail," you only fail in the eyes of men, not God. The Gospel will always be foolishness *to those who are perishing*, but to us who are being saved by it, it is the power of God (1 Cor. 1:18).

Guarding the truth,

Greg

Endnotes

1. Ben Sherwood, *The Survivors Club* (New York, Grand Central Publishers: 2009).

2. See Antony Flew, *There Is a God: How the World's Most Notorious Atheist Changed His Mind* (New York: HarperCollins, 2007).

3. The debate originally aired 12/30/09 on The Hugh Hewitt Show, Salem Radio Network.

4. See *Solid Ground*, Nov-Dec 2001, at str.org.

5. See Beckwith and Koukl, *Relativism: Feet Firmly Planted in Mid-Air* (Grand Rapids: Baker, 1998).

6. Clips of our engagement can be found readily on the internet.

7. The talk is called "Truth Is Not Ice Cream; Faith Is Not Wishing" and is part of the "Ambassador Basic Curriculum" (ABC) series, available at str.org.

8. Kelly Monroe, ed., *Finding God at Harvard* (Grand Rapids: Zondervan, 1996), 15.

9. Lawrence Hyman, "Whatever Happened to Atheism?," *Skeptic*, vol. 5, no. 2, 1997.

10. *Christianity Today*, December 2003.

11. Guinness and Seel, *No God But God: Breaking with the Idols of Our Age* (Chicago: Moody Press, 1992), 91.

12. Note, for example, John the Baptist's concern in Matthew 11:2-3.